DIGITAL CAMERA

FOR KID'S

USER GUIDE

A WELL DETAILED MANUAL TO HELP YOUR INFANT

BECOME PRO AT THEIR PRIME.

BY

BECKY SMITH

Copyright © 2024 **BECKY SMITH**

All rights reserved. This book is copyright and no part of it may be reproduced, distributed, or transmitted in any form or by any means, including photocopying, recording, or other electronic or mechanical methods, without the prior written permission of the publisher, except in the case of brief quotations embodied in critical reviews and certain other noncommercial uses permitted by copyright law.

Printed in the United States of America Copyright 2024

© **BECKY SMITH**

Table of Contents

INTRODUCION

In an age where technology shapes our world, empowering children with the skills to creatively navigate this digital landscape is a vital endeavor. "Through the Eyes of Young Shutterbugs: A Digital Camera Guide for Kids" invites young readers on an exciting journey into the captivating realm of photography. In this digital age, where every moment is a canvas waiting to be painted with pixels, this book serves as a trusty companion for budding photographers eager to explore the world through their own unique perspectives.

In a world saturated with screens, "Through the Eyes of Young Shutterbugs" offers a refreshing departure from passive consumption. With the ubiquity of smartphones and tablets, children often find themselves on the receiving end of images, videos, and games. This book, however, takes a different approach, putting the power of creation firmly into the hands of its readers. As they delve into the colorful pages of this guide, they'll uncover the magic behind photography, learning not only how to capture the world around them but also how to tell stories, evoke emotions, and freeze moments in time with the click of a button.

Designed to be more than just a technical manual, this book infuses the art of photography with the boundless imagination of young minds. Through interactive exercises, practical tips, and inspiring examples, young readers will embark on an educational adventure that blends technical know-how with creative expression. They will learn to wield digital cameras not merely as devices, but as extensions of their own curiosity and perspective, transforming everyday scenes into captivating narratives.

"Through the Eyes of Young Shutterbugs" understands that every child's journey into photography is unique. From candid snapshots of pets to sprawling landscapes and whimsical portraits of friends, this guide embraces the diverse interests and visions of its readers. Whether capturing a dreamy sunset or experimenting with playful angles, this book empowers young photographers to discover the world through a new lens—one that fosters artistic growth, self-confidence, and a lifelong appreciation for the beauty that surrounds us.

Join us as we embark on a visual expedition where the boundaries between the digital and the tangible blur, and where the voices of young shutterbugs resonate loudly through the pixels they capture. As we flip through the pages of this guide, it becomes evident that the next generation of photographers is ready not only to observe the world but to reimagine it one click at a time.

CHAPTER ONE

THE BASICS

The Light Connection

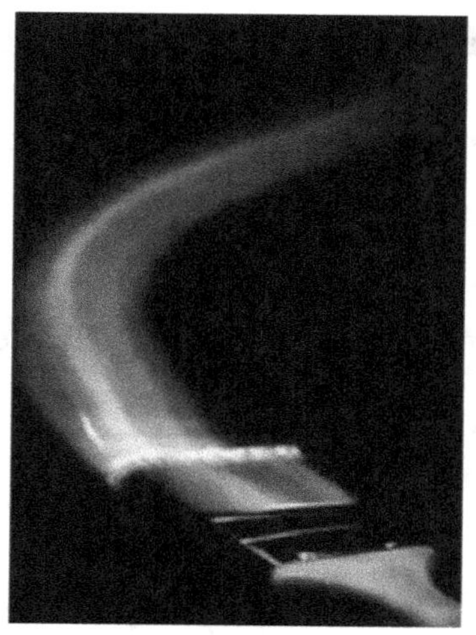

Since presumably the first persistent photograph was created in 1825 by French inventor Nicéphore Niépce, the expression "painting with light" has been used to describe photography. Light is essential to photography, but why is it referred to as "painting with light"? The word "photography" is derived from the Greek "photos," which means light, and "graph," which means to write or depict. (As a side note, there is also a type of photography known as light painting, in which you literally write with light; this is quite entertaining.) When painting an image, the medium may be oils, acrylics, or watercolors, but when photographing an image, the medium is light.

In a film camera, the image on the film is exposed by light. In your digital camera, the image is exposed on the image sensor. Without illumination, there is no image.

As you will see in this chapter, the way light descends on your subject—whether it be a person, animal, building, or flower—can make a significant difference in your photographs.

Natural Light:

Natural light is the ideal lighting source for photographs. One might assume that dazzling midday sunlight would be ideal for photographing, but the severe shadows at this time can really ruin a photo.

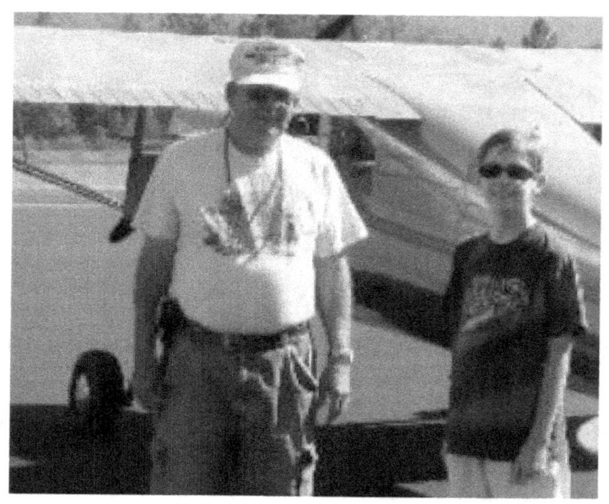

So when is the best moment to take your camera outdoors.

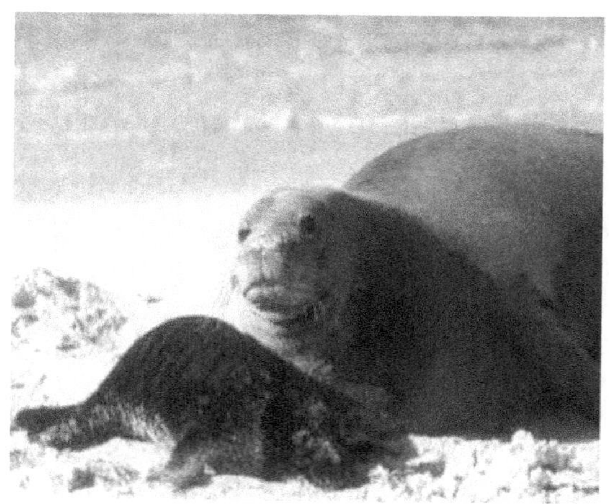

The Golden Period:

In general, the finest times of day for photography are when the sun

is low in the sky-approximately one hour after sunrise and one hour

before twilight, the heavens.

Photographers refer to these times as "Golden Hours" due to the fact that the sun at these times produces pleasant tones, long, delicate shadows.

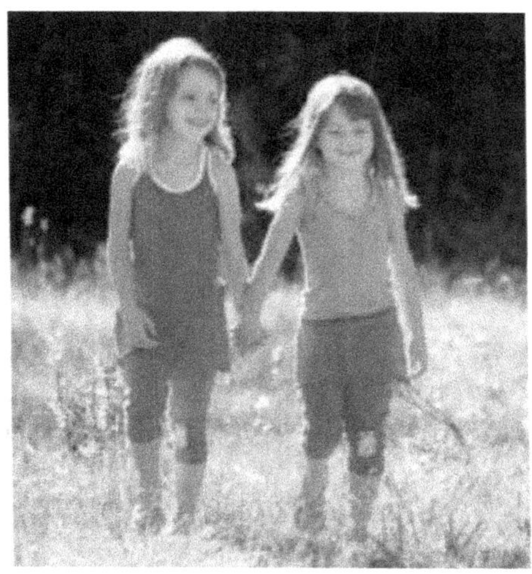

Remember that the higher the sun is in the sky, the greater the likelihood of intense shadows and overexposed highlights in your photographs.

Overcast:

The light from a cloudy atmosphere is also suitable for photography. This light is gentle and uniform. Even photography enthusiasts use specialized equipment indoors, such as diffusers and soft boxes, to replicate the gentle light of nature.

Don't let a cloudy day prevent you from enjoying the outdoors with your camera (unless, of course, the clouds are thunderclouds). If the sky is monotonous or glaringly colorless, attempt to exclude it as much as possible from your composition.

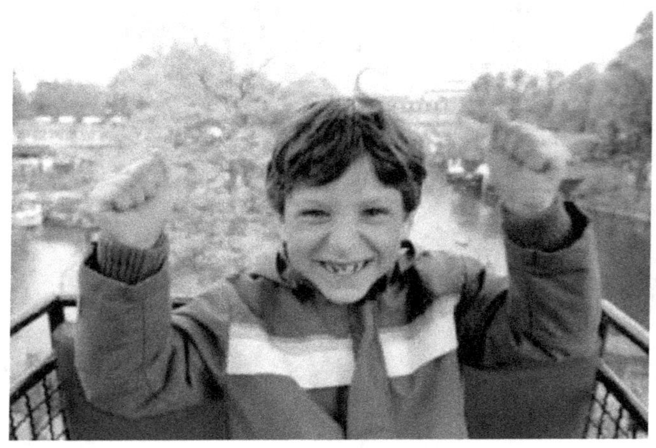

If you are photographing anything other than the sky, you will achieve an even illumination effect.

Back Light:

The effect of sunlight beaming from behind the subject can be quite appealing.

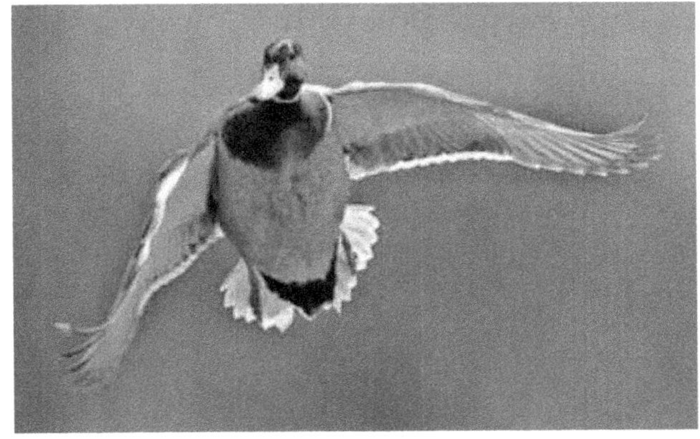

An excessive amount of illumination can obscure the subject and produce a silhouette. Occasionally, this is a positive thing.

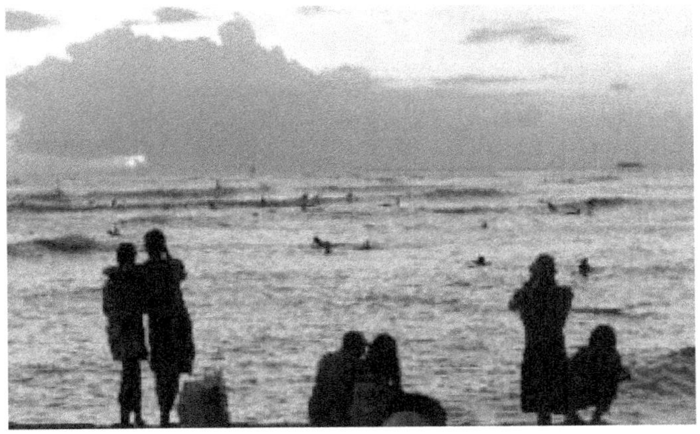

If you're shooting a picture with the sun behind the subject and you don't want the subject to be darkened, the light on your camera can save the day. Ensure that the subject is within the flash's range. Also, you must inform the camera that you intend to use the flash on a bright, sunny day. You can indicate this to your camera by setting illumination to "on" rather than "automatic."

Shooting into the light presents additional difficulties. It may result in lens reflections.

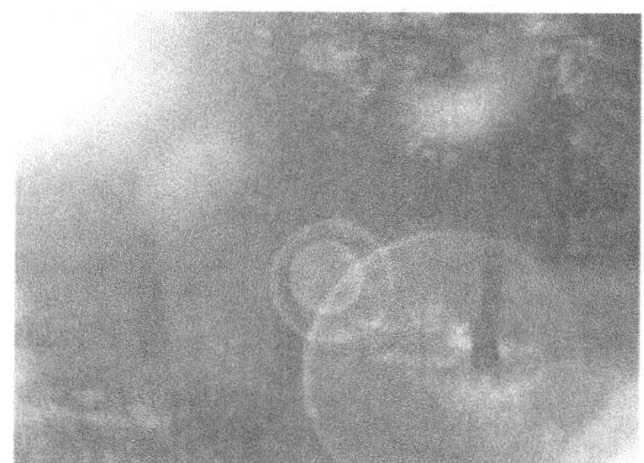

On photographs, lens flare appears as spectral patterns of the lens diaphragm.

To prevent lens glare, shield your camera's lens with a lens hood, your hand, or a hat with a stiff-brimmed brim.

Frontal Light:

When the sun is behind you and illuminating the front of the subject, we say that the subject is "front lit." This is the worst possible lighting for humans and animals, as they will grimace if they must face the sun.

Side Light:

This is often the best option for lighting angles, as side lighting can create a three-dimensional effect.

Shadows:

Shadows are not always a concern. Long shadows that extend across landscapes, for instance, add atmosphere to photographs. Shadows also accentuate forms, giving the image a more three-dimensional appearance. Therefore, professionals avoid using light directly on faces. Natural modeling is possible using natural light (or studio equipment). The darkness can be your ally.

ISO, Shutter Speed, and Aperture: The Exposure Triangle:

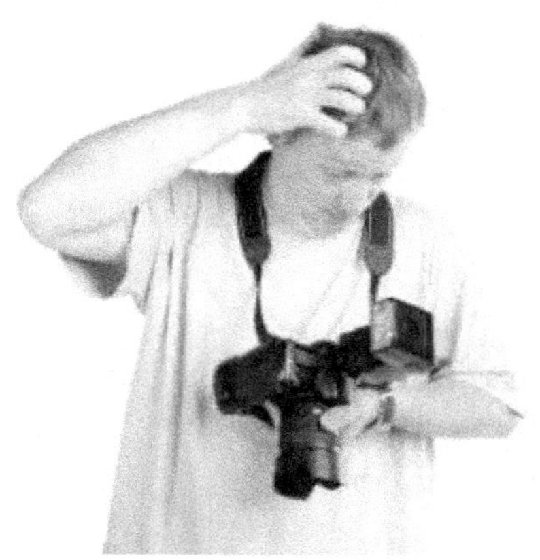

The technology behind photography appears to frighten more adults than the Bermuda Triangle. When you begin to impress your parents with your photographs, they may want to learn as well. Remember to exercise patience with them.

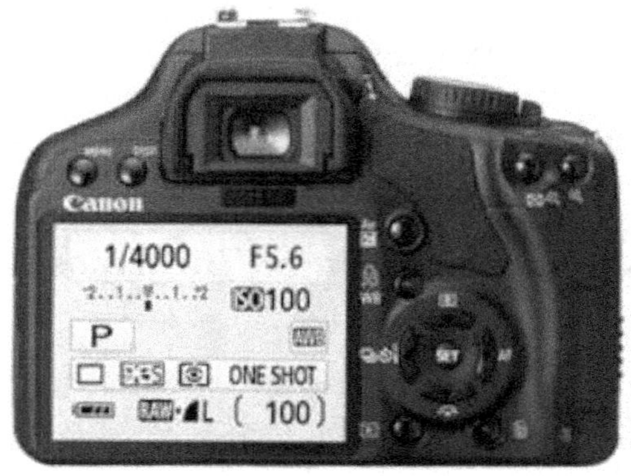

This chapter's content is not required to effectively utilize the remainder of the book. However, it can enhance your creativity. And if you ever decide to purchase an SLR, this will give you a head start on using it like a pro.

Exposure:

When you press the shutter release button, the amount of light that descends on the image sensor is the exposure. On the right, the image of the image sensor is not to scale. The majority are a fraction of an inch. When an excessive amount of light hits the sensor, the image is overexposed (too brilliant).

When there is insufficient light, a photograph is underexposed (too dark).

Aperture and shutter speed determine how much light reaches the image sensor.

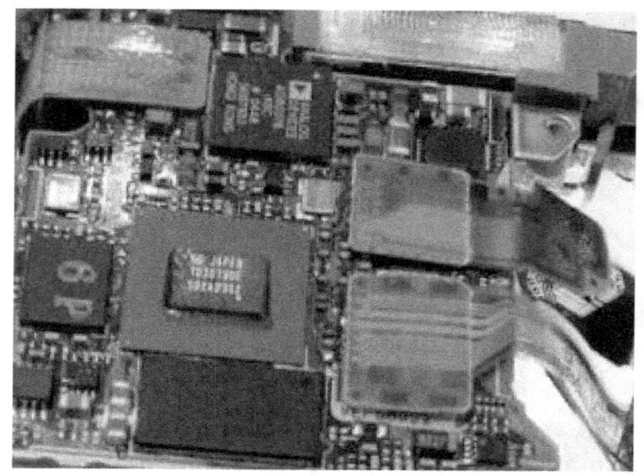

Aperture:

1. Designers of camera lenses modeled the aperture after the pupil of the human eye. Just as your iris dilates or constricts to allow more or less light through the pupils, so does the camera's lens diaphragm dilate or constrict to allow more or less light through the lens. The aperture measures the dimensions of this orifice.

1.

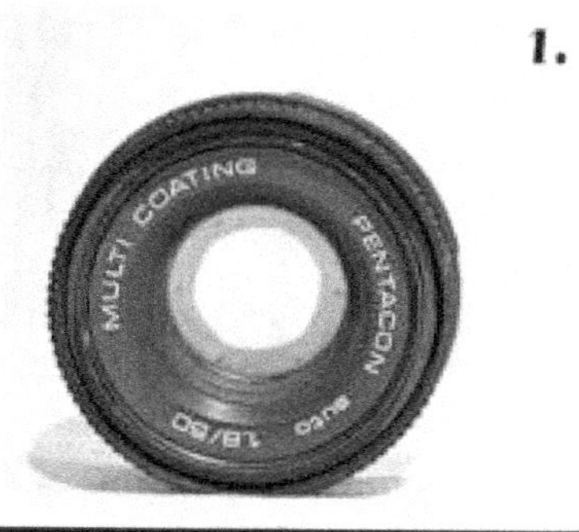

2. Aperture enables a photographer's (or a camera's)

If the exposure algorithm is set to autonomous, the exposure will increase.

Alternatively, reduce the amount of light that reaches the sensor. This helps determine the brightness or darkness of the image.

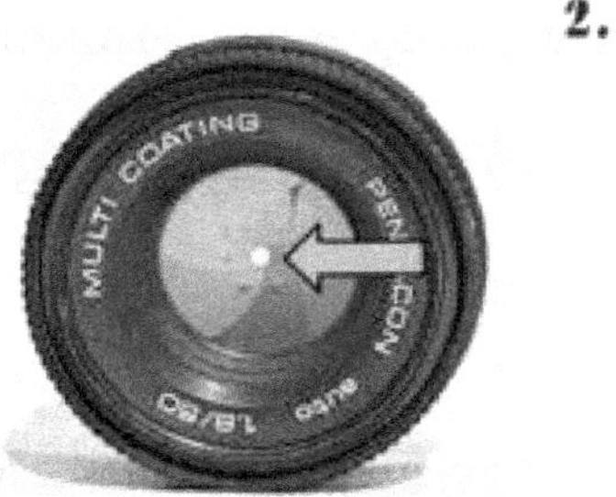

The aperture also serves another significant function. The aperture size determines the depth of field of an image.

Make a fist and hold it in front of your eye to get a sense of what this means. Then slowly open your hand. Observe when the opening in your hand is maximal.

Everything you see is in sharp focus. However, when the aperture is fully open, the object closest to you is sharper than the background.

This illustrates how depth of field determines the portion of a photograph that is in focus.

A narrow aperture is ideal for landscape photography, in which the entire scene should be in focus. When you want only the subject to be in focus, such as in a picture of your dog gazing curiously at the camera, a wide aperture is ideal.

A few cameras feature an aperture-priority mode. This enables you to determine the aperture within the camera's f-stop (or f-stop, for short) range. Contrary to popular belief, the larger the f-stop number, the smaller the aperture. This is because the numbers represent ratios rather than whole integers.

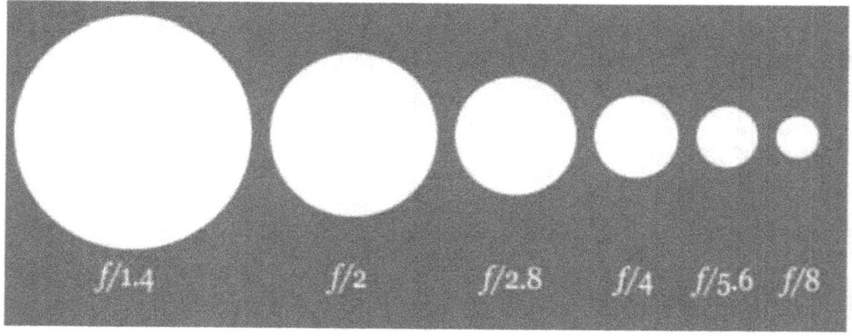

This book will emphasize modes, such as athletic mode, over manual settings. Nonetheless, if your camera has an aperture priority setting, you must remember that the greater the f-stop number, the greater the depth of field.

When you set the aperture, the camera will attempt to set the shutter speed so that the exposure is correct (not too black or too light).

Shutter Velocity:

While the aperture regulates how much light descends on the image sensor at once, the shutter speed determines how long the camera lets light in.

The most typical shutter velocities range from 1/500 to 1/60 seconds, or 1/500th to 1/60th of a second. Many digital cameras feature a priority shutter speed setting. If it does, you can select rates (within the camera's range) to achieve the desired effect.

If, unlike the majority of point-and-shoot digital cameras, yours does not, you may have settings such as Sports Mode that instruct the camera to use a specific shutter speed. If you choose your own shutter speed, bear in mind that you will likely need a tripod or other camera support for shutter velocities less than 1/60. When the shutter is open for so long, the camera captures even the slightest movement. This results in the photo being out of focus or blurry.

Set the camera's shutter priority to a rapid speed or the sports mode to capture action. For instance, soccer requires anywhere between 1/250 and 1/500. To photograph a pet calmly seated, set the shutter speed to approximately 1/125 (or use sports mode, as in the image to the right), as pets rarely sit absolutely still.

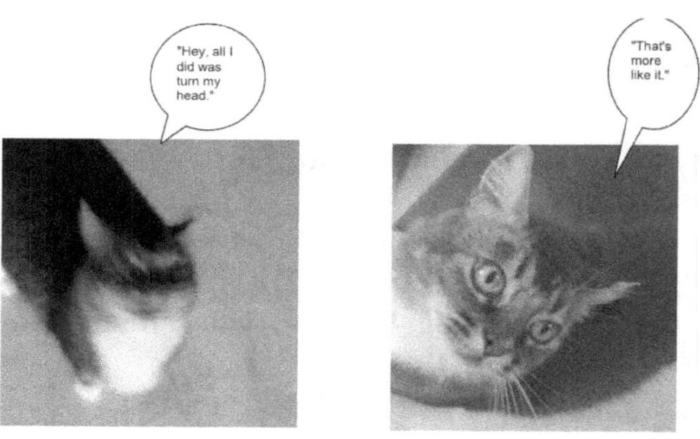

When you examine photographs of early 19th-century cities, you will notice that there are almost never any individuals present. It required so much time for a

People had passed through the scene without being captured by the camera because the shutter speed at the time was so sluggish.

During the 19th century, posing for photographs was no picnic, as exposures took several minutes. No wonder there are so many frowns in ancient photographs! They posed for several minutes in the early 19th century. Neither did the fashion of the time likely serve to brighten them up.

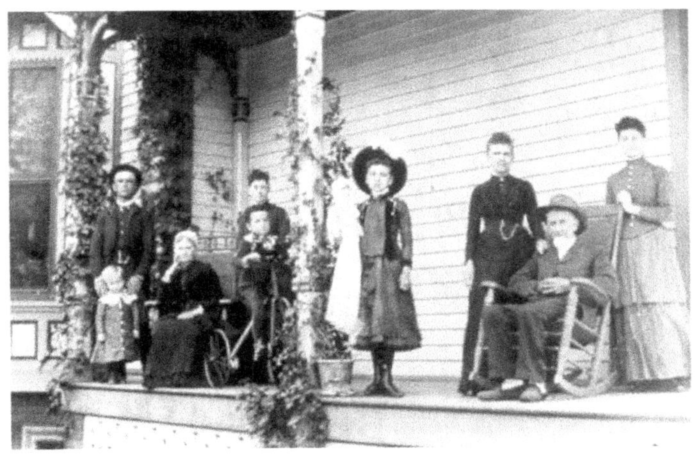

ISO:

In digital photography, ISO refers to the image sensor's sensitivity. When using a manual setting, you can make the sensor more or less sensitive to light by increasing or decreasing the ISO. With SLR cameras, you can significantly increase the ISO to get sharper photos at indoor events where illumination is prohibited. Setting the ISO above 100 on cameras with smaller image sensors than SLRs can result in digital dithering in the image. The appearance of digital noise is granular, but unlike film images, the grain contains minuscule colored specks.

With the majority of cameras, the lowest ISO setting is optimal. Some photographers use a higher ISO and then noise reduction software to smooth out the uneven hues. such as Noise Ninja.

Composing Your Shot

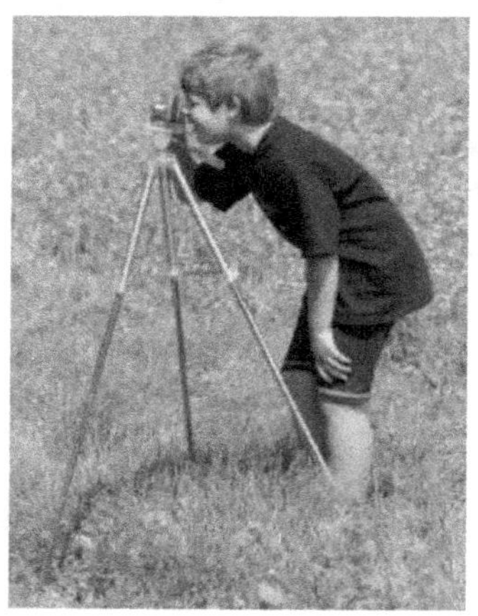

After lighting, composition is the most essential element for capturing great photographs.

Most images in photo albums are black-and-white. photographic images. A snapshot is an unplanned photograph. a lot of forethought. It's as easy as pointing and shooting. Taking a number of photographs usually yields one or two excellent images. But it's a game of numbers. In contrast, composing an image prior to striking the shutter button allows you to exercise creative control. By doing so, you significantly increase the number of pictures that leave your peers awestruck. This is how.

Fill Your Frame:

This is one of the simplest ways to add appeal to a photograph. For instance, if you are photographing your dog in the backyard, only include the dog and not the entire backyard. When a document contains an excessive amount of information, it is deemed excessive. photograph, the subject becomes obscured. When the dog is sharing space with the barbecue, swing, sprinkler, picnic table, and Aunt Betty, it is difficult to discern the dog's characteristics. You get the picture.

It is possible that the circle or rectangle engraved onto the glass of many viewfinders confuses the majority of individuals, causing them to not complete their frame. Your photographs extend to the very boundaries of the viewfinder. Another reason for all this debris (I know, Aunt Betty is not litter, but this is a photography term) is the photographer's attempt to include too much.

Consider this before composing your photograph: What is the most essential element you wish to highlight? If it is your dog, move closer or zoom in until he occupies the viewfinder or LCD screen. You can always photograph Aunt Betty and the yard in the future.

How do you, therefore, occupy your frame?

1. Utilize your zoom (optical is optimal, as you will see in the following chapter).

2. Utilize your legs to approach the subject closer.

3. Use your photo editor's crop function; this is the least preferable option, as extensive cropping degrades image quality. This is acceptable if you only need a modest image.

Simplify: Get Rid of Clutter:

Remember how you feel when you look at your bedroom after you've cleaned it up? In the language of photography, debris refers to anything that detracts from the subject of your photograph. Neither is it very restful.

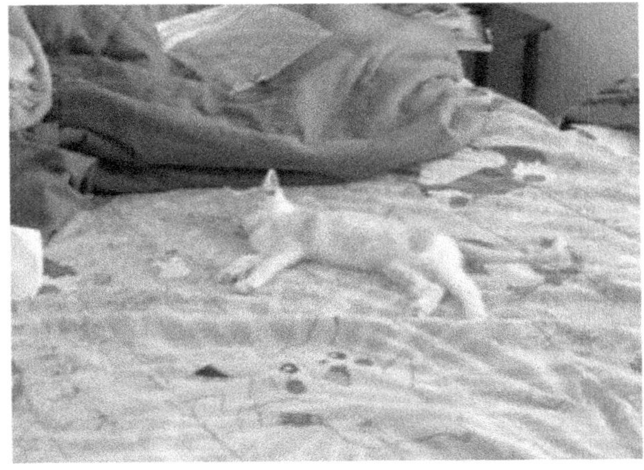

There are numerous distractions here. Also, it is difficult to determine whether Simba or Pikachu are the subjects of this photograph.

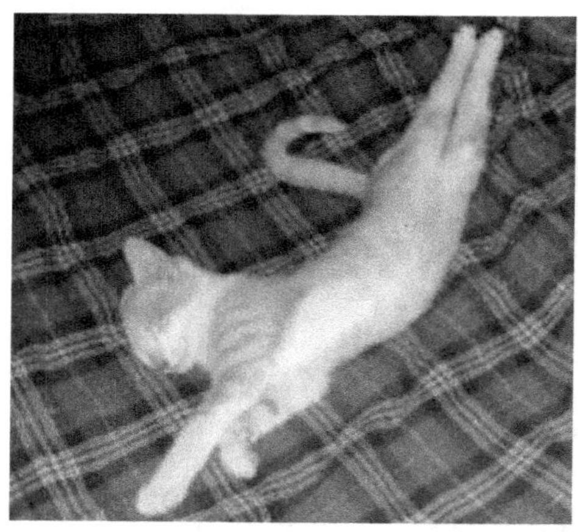

There's no question who the protagonist is here! (Good stretching, Simba)

Before you begin to compose your image, examine the surrounding area. Then relocate or conceal the debris.

Check the playback mode for surprises, such as a branch emerging out of your friend's cranium, after taking the photo. Due to digital technology, you can delete

Request that your friend move slightly and fire again. There is not always time to clear the scene before filming. For instance, if you have your camera available when your sibling does something adorable or your companion does something silly, all you need to do is point and shoot.

Photo editors such as Gimp (free) and Photoshop Elements can be used to eradicate clutter later. Advanced users can even alter backgrounds entirely.

Not all debris constitutes true disorder. Occasionally, the subject of your photograph will include additional elements. As an illustration, a portrait of a matriarch. Whoever enjoys horticulture may be photographed in a garden with blooms surrounding her and a watering can in hand. The flowers and watering can are not debris in these instances. They are included in the subject. The subject is Grandma with her watering can and flowers.

Filling the frame with your subject also provides a closer perspective with more details. However, remember that your subject need not always occupy the frame. As you will see below, vacant space afforded by elements such as a meadow or the sky often produces a pleasing effect.

Law of Thirds:

When snapping a quick photo, we typically position the subject dead center. In professional photographs, however, the subject is rarely centered within the frame.

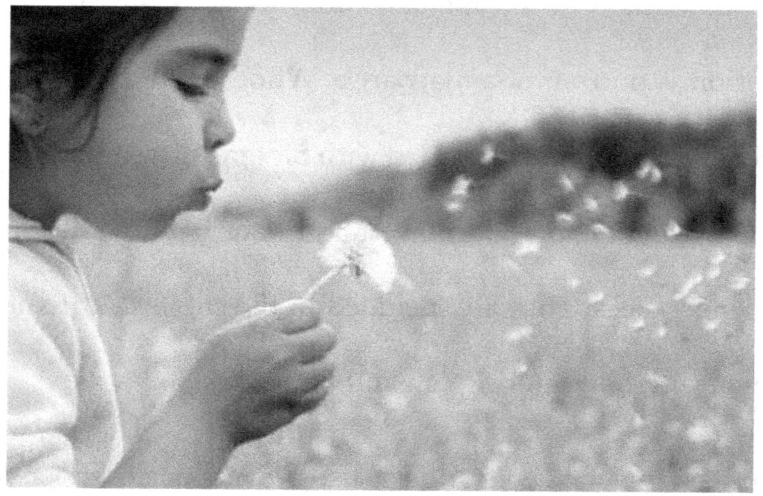

This is due to the fact that professionals utilize traditional composition techniques, specifically the Rule of Thirds. The fundamental concept behind the rule of thirds is to divide an image into nine equal portions using six evenly spaced lines. Some cameras have a feature that displays a "tic-tac-toe" grid over the image during preview.

The objective is to position the subject on one of the intersections

or one of the lines.

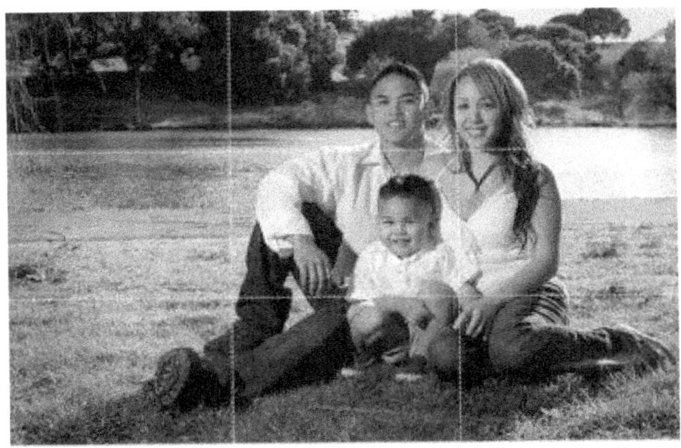

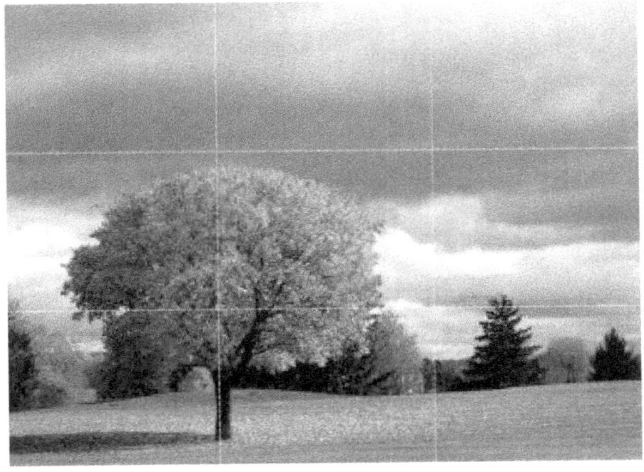

Utilizing the Rule of Thirds requires some adjustment, but with

practice, it becomes second nature. As evidenced by the portrait of

the family, precise alignment is not required. The concept is to center your subject in one of the outer third spaces, as opposed to the bull's-eye.

The Rule of Thirds works well in the majority of situations, but sometimes positioning a subject in the center of an image creates a striking image.

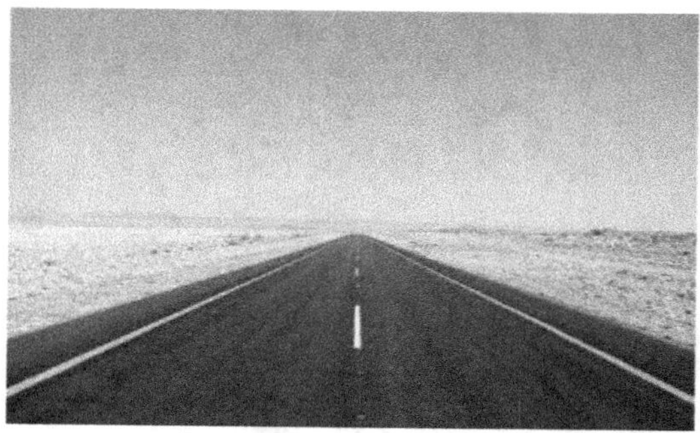

Contrast:

The greater the contrast, the brighter the brights and the darker the darks. Contrast is not required for an excellent photograph, but it does make images stand out.

In a photograph, contrast may consist of a blue sky and dark green trees, shadows and highlights on a rock formation, or a white racecar on a black track.

Once you develop the habit of searching for it, contrast is easy to locate. All of this contributes to the development of a photographer's vision.

Angle:

Do not fall into the common practice of capturing photographs only from eye level. This can become tedious. Consider adjusting your eye level by sitting. lying on the ground or standing on a step or perch. Take the majority of pictures of people and animals at their eye level.

Consider holding the camera vertically.

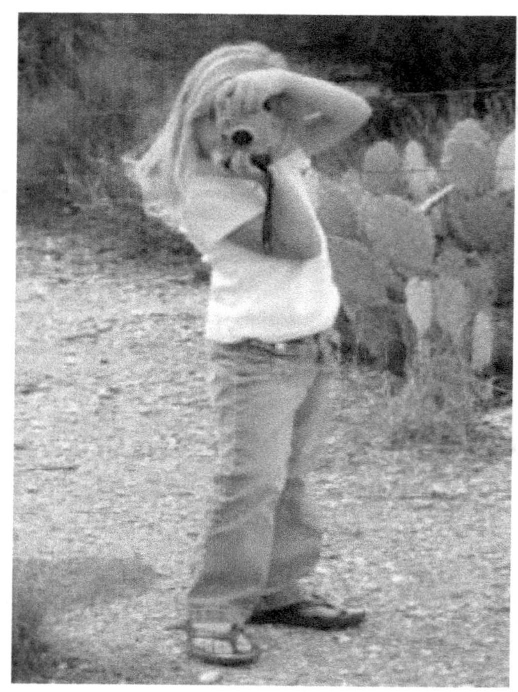

Take one of each and compare the results!

Additionally, be creative and take a few photos from an unusual angle. Keep in mind that offset does not work well when there is a horizon or a building in the photograph, but it can be fascinating when photographing humans or animals.

Have some joy!

Digital Cameras And Accessories

This provides an overview of the functions. Before purchasing a new camera, deciding on accessories, or compiling a Christmas list, it is beneficial to peruse this article.

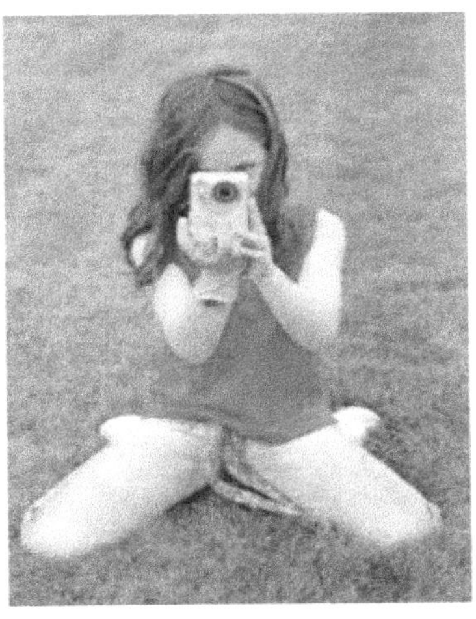

Digital SLR (occasionally abbreviated as DSLR):

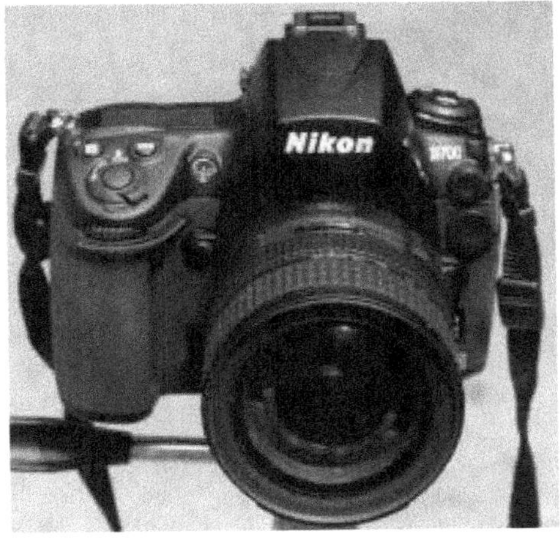

The majority of this book's readers will not possess this form of camera. Digital SLR cameras are expensive and were almost exclusively used by professionals until recently.

The cost of entry-level SLRs, such as the Canon Rebel, has decreased. However, when purchasing an SLR, you must also purchase lenses. The above camera has a lens, but it did not come that way from the camera store.

The camera body is followed by the purchase of lenses. Some do include a stock lens—a rudimentary introductory lens. If you want telephoto, you cannot simply magnify by pressing a switch; you need a telephoto lens. These are available in a variety of sizes to meet the requirements of photographers.

On the positive side, there are telephoto lenses that allow you to take a close-up of a bird perched at the summit of a tree or a football player in the end zone from the 50-yard line of the stands. SLR cameras are compatible with sophisticated accessories like external illumination.

SLRs are ideal for capturing action photos in low-light situations where illumination is either not permitted or impossible to reach. And they are quick.

The single-lens reflex technology does not allow for a preview mode, so you must compose your photos through the viewfinder. And few SLR cameras have a movie mode.

It's a great camera to upgrade to if you discover you enjoy photography and wish to progress. Many begin with a camera body and basic lens and gradually upgrade to larger lenses.

Digital point-and-shoot (P&S) cameras

Compacts:

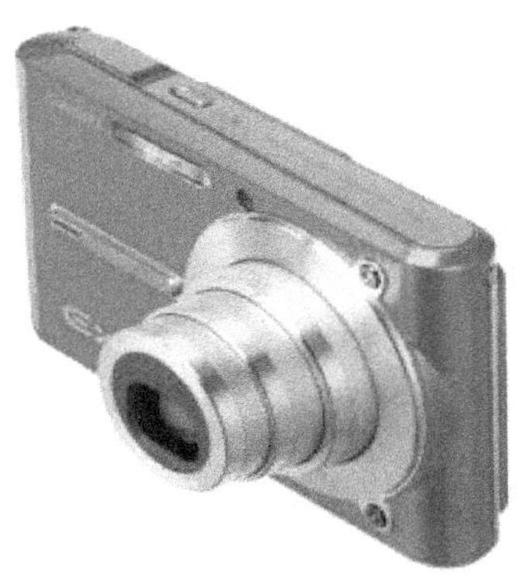

For good reason, digital compacts are the most ubiquitous cameras in the Western world. They are compact and lightweight. Numerous professionals with a costly SLR and a large case of lenses carry a compact camera in their pocket because it is so portable and takes such high-quality photographs. Pocket-sized compacts are commonly referred to as subcompacts.)

As previously mentioned, compacts have a few features that most SLRs lack: movie mode and LCD display

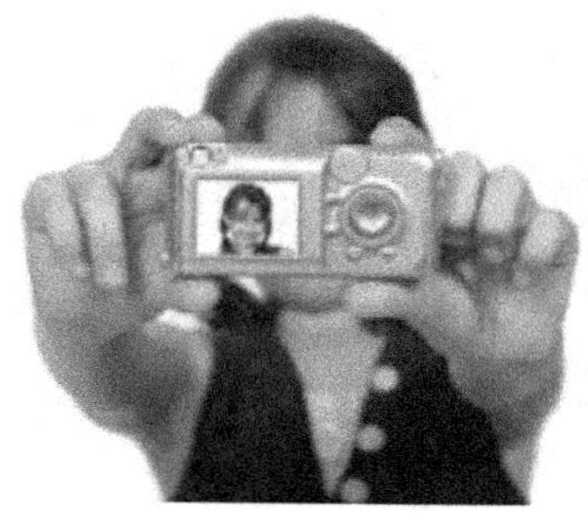

Even though you can simply aim and fire with these cameras, you will learn much more.

There are a variety of modes to choose from, and many cameras also offer manual controls. Many have more capabilities than the vast majority ever use! If your camera has optical magnification, you can also take excellent telephoto photos.

Bridge Camcorders:

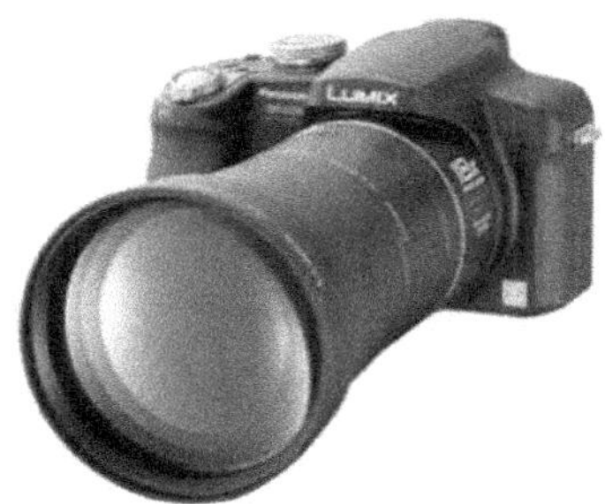

These digital cameras serve as a bridge between compacts and SLRs. They are also referred to as prosumer cameras (a term derived from professional, as in the majority of SLR users, and consumer, as in non-professional camera purchasers).

Almost all bridge cameras are more expensive than most compacts but less expensive than most SLRs.

They have larger sensors and more megapixels than the majority of compact cameras. Due to the larger sensor, ISO can be increased more than with a compact camera (though not nearly as much as with an SLR). Numerous bridge cameras feature hot shoe compatibility with external flashes. As with compacts, but unlike the majority of SLRs, they have a movie mode and an LCD for composing photos.

Numerous are ultra-zooms. This means that their optical magnification ranges are between 10x and 20x.

In addition, bridge cameras have nearly as many manual controls as SLR cameras.

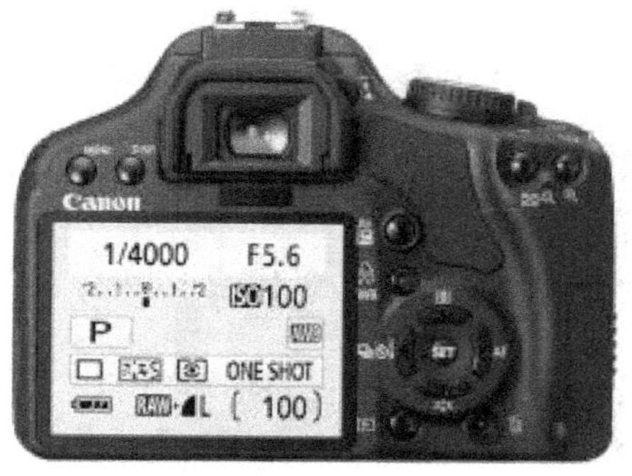

Camcorders:

The good news is that if you are interested in shooting movies and purchasing a point-and-shoot camera, these topics are not covered in this book. With 30 frames per second (fps) and 640 by 480 resolution, the majority of point-and-shoots manufactured after 2007 are able to capture quite respectable video.

Accessories

- **Carrying Case:**

These vary in size, shape, and pigment. Some are softer than others. Also available are hermetic and impermeable options. Many contain space for an additional memory card and spare batteries.

- **Memory Cards:**

Also known as memory cards and memory sticks, these are the equivalent of film for digital cameras. They are removable and store the photographs captured by the camera. Storage cards are rewritable, so you can delete and reuse them after transferring images to your computer.

Consult your camera's manual to determine the type. The more memory, the more photos can be stored on the device.

- **Charging Batteries:**

This can significantly reduce battery costs. Some cameras include a compact charger that is ideal for charging two to four batteries. Additionally, it is prudent to carry an additional set of batteries. Check your manual for the sort of AAs that your vehicle takes.

- **The tripod:**

If you take photographs with shutter speeds less than 1/60, you will need some form of camera support. The majority of cameras have a threaded cavity into which the tripod head inserts. The more sturdy a tripod is, the better.

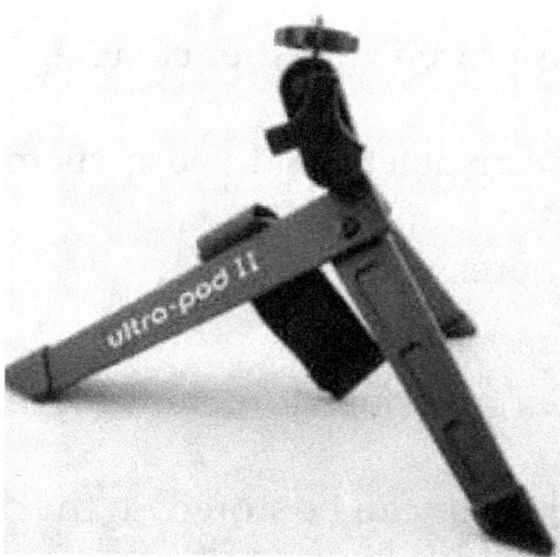

A portable tripod that can be set up on a surface can be just as stable.

There are numerous alternatives to tripods, such as photography beanbags, a folded windbreaker, and a large sack of rice, that can be used to stabilize the camera.

Getting Acquainted With Your Camera

Camera Parts

- **The viewfinder:**

This is located in the upper portion of the camera. It is the component you hold to your eye to compose your shot when the LCD screen is not available. Unless you are using an SLR, the viewfinder may only display 80 to 90 percent of the actual image captured by the camera.

The viewfinder is nevertheless useful. Sometimes the reflection on the LCD makes it difficult to compose a photo. Occasionally, you may need to place the camera against your face to stabilize it.

- **LCD:**

This miniature monitor on point-and-shoot cameras (and a few SLRs) displays the complete composition in real time. While the LCD screen is nearly ideal for assessing composition and framing, it is less than ideal for determining exposure. It causes photographs to appear livelier to the photographer than they actually are.

After taking a photo, adjust the screen from preview to playback to determine if the image was successful. Numerous cameras allow you to view images in groups of thumbnails that, when clicked, expand to their full dimension.

Some cameras are equipped with LCDs that pivot and/or revolve. This makes it simpler to capture images from various angles.

- **Camera Release:**

This is the button you press to snap a photograph. Keep your forearms down (no chicken wings), keep your ankles apart, maintain a sturdy grip, and strike the shutter button (don't pummel) to prevent camera movement, which can result in indistinct photographs. Remain still until the photograph has been captured. This could require a few seconds. The light will signify its completion.

- **Lens:**

The lens, composed of optical glass or a comparable material, captures and focuses light rays to create an image on the sensor.

- **The audio:**

If your camera has audio recording capabilities, you can record notes (or other noises).

with an image you capture. The movie modes of the majority of cameras enable you to record audio while filming. The microphone is concealed within, but you will notice a collection of pinprick-sized openings. Numerous cameras feature a port for attaching an external microphone. When you upload images to your computer, the accompanying audio files are automatically included.

- **The movie:**

Most point-and-shoot cameras have a button or dial setting for switching to video recording without entering the menu. This mode is represented by an image of a film camera. The recording duration will vary depending on the camera and memory card used. Movies consume significantly more memory than still images.

- **Independent Timer:**

This is a wonderful feature to have if you want to take a picture with yourself in it, such as one of you and your closest friend or your family.

Instead of handing over your camera to someone who may not know how to operate it, you can compose the image, set the timer, and then leap into the photo. You have between 2 and 10 seconds, depending on your camera's parameters and the self-timer, so move quickly.

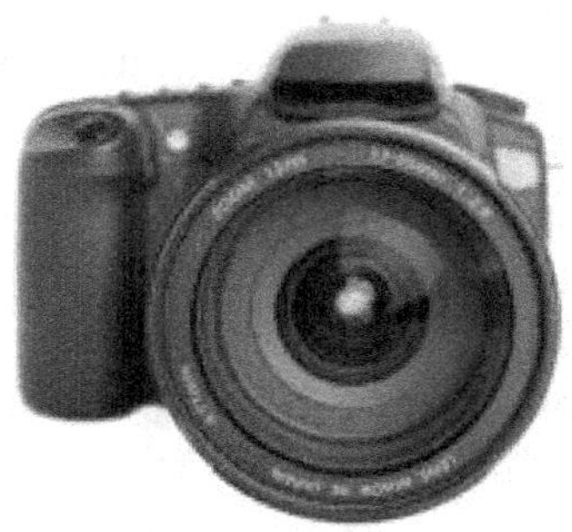

- **Zoom:**

A point-and-shoot camera may have either a fixed or telescopic lens. The telescopic lens functions similarly to binoculars. It magnifies the subject so that you can approach it without moving an inch. This can be very useful if you want to take unguarded photos of your friends or capture close-ups of untamed animals, such as a crocodile at the zoo or a frightened insect.

Do not believe anyone who claims digital magnification is equivalent to optical zoom. Comparing optical and digital magnification is like comparing pears and oranges, YouTube and IMAX, poodles and Rottweilers, and so on.

If your camera has both modes, disable the digital mode. You will have a shorter range, but the quality will be superior. This is due to the fact that optical magnification alters the quantity of scene that falls on the image sensor. As the image enters the lens, the lens functions as a magnifying glass before the image reaches the sensor. Every pixel in the image contains unique data, ensuring that the final image is crisp and distinct.

Digital magnification, however, diminishes the quality of the image. You can obtain a passable image with digital zoom for very small prints and email, but don't push it to its limit, as quality degrades with each increase in magnification. This is due to the interpolation it employs: it extracts a portion of the image resting on the sensor and enlarges it by adding new pixels to occupy the sensor. The interpolated image has fewer distinct pixels than one captured with optical magnification. Digital zoom produces the same effect as cropping and then enlarging an image in a photo-editing program.

How do you determine the magnification range of your camera? There is typically a number followed by an x on the camera's body. Example: 5x indicates that the subject appears five times closer. When purchasing a camera, you can determine its optical and/or digital magnification by reading the specifications.

Flash-on-Camera - A P&S will either have an integrated flash or a pop-up flash.

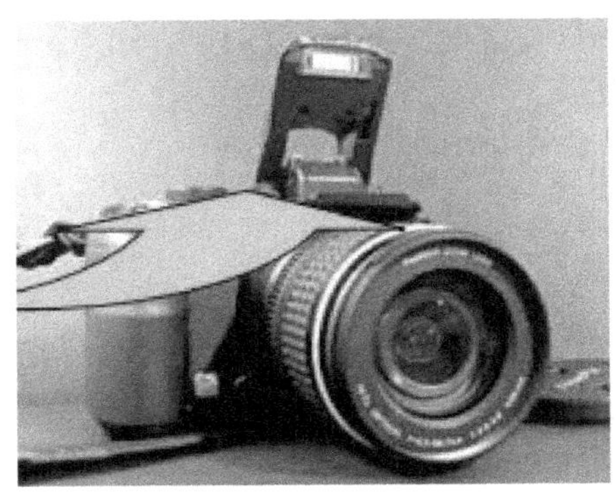

Neither is the optimal principal source of illumination. On-camera illumination casts strong shadows and gives subjects a somewhat two-dimensional appearance. The majority of people utilize it, but experts avoid it like pestilence. In most instances, this is the case.

Even professional photographers will use it when photographing outdoors when shadows are cast by natural light. When the camera's flash is used in this manner, it is referred to as "fill flash" or "fill-in flash" because it fills in the light gaps left by the primary light source.

For optimal results, it is essential not to exceed the recommended flash photography distance, so consult your camera's manual. This light will only reach a certain distance. Therefore, you cannot rely on it unless your subject is within a few feet. Then, what do you use indoors? Typically, natural light and/or indoor illumination are effective (more on this later).

Terms to learn:

When you start using these phrases, your parents and friends will think you're an expert! Even better, you will have a greater understanding of how to operate your camera.

- **JPEG and JPG:**

This is the most prevalent image storage format used by digital cameras. Either "JPEG" or "JPG" is the acceptable spelling. JPGs are compressed versions of the images you create. Most cameras use the JPEG file format. Some, particularly SLRs, utilize the RAW format. With RAW format, there is no compression, so you can capture larger, higher-quality images, but they require an enormous quantity of memory card space.

- **Pixels:**

The image sensor of your camera contains millions of pixels (picture elements). Each pixel generates a minute electrical charge in response to the light it detects. The greater the number of pixels on an image sensor, the greater the camera's prospective resolution.

- **Resolution:**

This value indicates the number of pixels utilized to acquire an image. Resolution ranges from low (640 x 480) to high (and beyond 2592 x 1944). Multiplying the two numbers and dividing by one million determines the number of megapixels. In other terms, 2592 x 1994 corresponds to 5,038,848 pixels, or 5 megapixels. With 5 megapixels, your camera has a high resolution. Different resolutions are suitable for various applications. If your camera allows you to choose between low and high resolution, you may want to select low if the photos will only be used for emailing or website pages (600 x 1200 to 2048 x 1536 pixels). After all, nobody enjoys having to navigate to view images in email attachments or wait eternally for a page to load.

Nonetheless, if you intend to publish some of your photos or upload larger versions to a website so that thumbnails will link to them, here are some guidelines:

- 3 megapixels produce fine 4x6 images, acceptable 5x7s, and, depending on the camera, possibly even reasonable 6x9 or 8x10s.

- 4 megapixels produce exceptional 4x6s, very respectable 5x7s and 6x9s, and acceptable 8x10s.

- 5 megapixels yields stunning 8x10s and respectable 11x14s.

- 6 megapixels: provides superb photographs up to 11 x 14 inches and respectable poster size (particularly if your camera's sensor is 2/3 inch or larger).

Images with higher resolutions are more clear and distinct. And if you have a photo that is too large, you can reduce its size through photo editing. If you have a photo that is smaller than you desire, you cannot enlarge it without making it appear terrible.

If you want to crop your photo, you will have ample space to do so without losing too many pixels if you use a high JPG quality setting.

What is the drawback of capturing in high JPG? The memory device will fill up more quickly. Consider thoroughly what you intend to do with your photographs. Then examine your camera's megapixel count and the chart above. Consider the capacity of your memory device. Perform some calculations and determine which path to take. If you have access to an additional memory card, you will be able to make fewer difficult decisions.

If you are running out of space and do not have an additional memory card, switch to playback and examine your photos to determine which ones you wish to delete.

- **ISO:**

This metric evaluates the image sensor's light sensitivity. You obtain the highest image quality by setting your camera's ISO to its lowest setting. There are instances when a higher ISO is advantageous, but if you're not using a DSLR, it can result in digital noise. For the majority of compacts, 50 or 100 should be selected.

- **Automatic focusing:**

The majority of digital cameras feature autofocus. Most settings are preset by default. In autofocus mode (AF), the camera focuses on what it determines to be the image's primary subject.

The majority of cameras have center focus, which means the camera automatically focuses on whatever is in the middle of the viewfinder or LCD frame. If the You can fool your camera's autofocus if your subject is not in the center, which is often the case.

This is how.

Your photograph should be composed so that the subject is centered. Then press the shutter trigger halfway and maintain that position. The camera's focus will be locked. On most cameras, this is indicated by a green indicator.

Then, while continuing to hold the shutter button halfway down, move the camera to the desired position and press the shutter button the remainder of the descent. In a flash! Your camera's autofocus is responsible for focusing.

Default Modes:

Under each of the following camera modes is a section titled "How It Works." You do not need to comprehend how these modes work in order to use them, but understanding the "why" will increase your knowledge of photography and make it simpler to use manual controls, should you choose to advance to those.

Additionally, understanding how something operates allows one to be more inventive and resourceful. For instance, you may select a particular mode to obtain a camera to perform a task that would otherwise require manual controls. In other words, as you've likely heard from numerous instructors, "Knowledge is power!"

Mode for Sports (or Action):

Look for the icon of a running person. Herein is the When you want to pause action rather than obscure it, use this mode. In Sports Mode, you can capture an image of your companion diving into home plate or your dog pursuing a ball.

- **How it operates:**

In sports mode, the camera's shutter speed is increased. But when it closes more quickly, less light enters. Therefore, this mode functions best in bright environments, such as outdoors. Some point-and-shoot cameras feature a shutter priority mode. This allows you to control the shutter speed while the camera determines the aperture based on the amount of light it detects.

Mode Burst/Continuous:

As the name suggests, this preset instructs the camera to take multiple shots in rapid succession (usually 5 or 6). Then you can decide which ones to retain. With film cameras, this feature was exclusive to SLRs. Many digital point-and-shoot cameras have this feature. If your camera has this mode, it can be very useful when attempting to capture a candid image of an active subject or when photographing sports.

- **How it works:**

This function establishes a fast shutter speed and uses buffering so that it doesn't have to pause and record each image to the camera's hard drive or memory card. memory card prior to the next. There is a brief delay after the flurry of photos before the camera allows you to fire again because it must transfer the images from the buffer to memory.

The portrait:

Almost every camera has this feature. This mode enables you to take portraits with a clear foreground and a blurred backdrop, as depicted by a head-and-shoulders image of a person. How much it can diminish The background, depending on your camera and how far behind your subject the background is, should be at least 10 feet.

- **How it operates:**

The camera enlarges the aperture and determines the optimal shutter speed to bring the subject into precise focus while blurring the background.

Landscape:

This popular mode is portrayed on the camera with an image of a mountain peak (or a figure 8 if your camera calls it "Infinity"). However, landscape mode is not only for landscapes. It's also for seascapes and cityscapes, or any photograph in which you want everything to be in focus, not just the subject. particular subject.

- **How it operates:**

The camera reduces the aperture to enhance the depth of field so that both nearby and distant objects are in focus.

Macro:

This is typically represented by a tulip-like floral. The majority of cameras have it. Macro photography permits extremely close-up shots. If you were to capture a close-up photo of a flower or insect using automatic focus, the image would be out of focus and possibly blurry. How near can one get? Approximately one inch to one foot, depending on the camera; consult the manual.

- **How it operates:**

The camera employs an extremely wide aperture in order to focus up close.

Evening or dusk portrait:

Numerous cameras feature this mode. Typically depicted by a person and a star on a dark background, this is used for, yep, people after dark, and specifically with illuminated backgrounds, such as carnivals or nightclubs.Christmas lights.

- **How it operates:**

The setting employs both illumination and a delayed shutter speed to capture the beautiful lighting. Due to the sluggish shutter speed, you may require additional support for the camera, such as a tripod, to prevent dithering. Or obscure it for an amusing special effect.

The fireworks:

This allows you to capture the vivid colors and luminosity of pyrotechnics. It can also be used in circumstances where you want to capture brilliant lights after dusk, such as carnival lights or lightning (but don't go outside or near a window if there's a possibility of lightning striking nearby a mile is much too close ask your parents first!).

- **How it operates:**

For a narrow aperture, the camera powers off the flash and sets autofocus to landscape or infinity. In order to prevent overexposure of the pyrotechnics, it also disables automatic exposure compensation and reduces the shutter speed and ISO. That requires a lot of adjustment!

White Balance Settings:

Generally, when striking in full automatic white balance mode eliminates unnatural tones and tints so that objects that appear white in real life appear white in photographs. Occasionally, however, the camera fails to produce the desired color. This is where settings such as cloudy, sunset, etc. enter into play. The setting instructs the camera to alter its white balance and contrast to capture the scene as accurately as possible.

- **Having clouds:** This can also be used in shaded locations and provides additional heating. counterbalance the overcast day's dim illumination.

- **The element tungsten:** This white balance correction adds blue tones to counteract the yellow tint that these types of indoor bulbs produce.

- **What is fluorescent:** Contrary to tungsten lighting, fluorescent lighting imparts a bluish hue, which this setting compensates for.

- **Sunset and dawn:** When using this setting, the camera makes adjustments. White balance is used to emphasize the pleasant tones of a twilight or sunrise. This increases the saturation of the photograph's pleasant tones. It also reduces the aperture to ensure that distant objects remain in focus. Nearby objects are crisp and distinct. This mode is identical to landscape, with added richness.

- **Beach versus snow:** Oftentimes, when photographing pristine white snow or when photographing a white sand beach, the camera reduces the brightness because it deems it too brilliant. This results in drab beaches and blue or gray snow.

  These modes indicate that snow or sand should be brilliant.

- If your camera lacks the desired white balance setting, you can attempt to fool it. "Cloudy" will give tenderness to an image, while "tungsten" will introduce blue. Do not fear experimentation. No worries if you don't have these parameters. When modifying on a computer, you can customize the hues.

Reduces red eyes:

When a camera's light beams directly into a the crimson blood vessels in the rear of a person's eye are illuminated. Red-eye reduction on a camera functions by constricting the pupils eyes of the subject so that they do not let in all that light.

How does your camera control the pupils of your subject? Does this begin to sound like strange science? You may have performed an experiment on your own pupils by entering a dark room with a mirror, turning on the light, and glancing quickly to observe your pupils contract. When "red eye reduction" is turned "on," the camera is instructed to illuminate twice. The first flash (similar to turning on a light in a dark room) causes the pupils to constrict, and the second flash illuminates the image. If this does not work, crimson can usually be readily removed with a photo editor.

Face Identification:

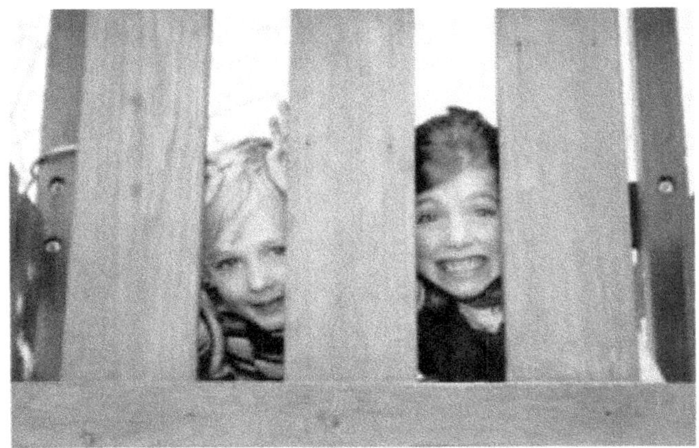

This enables your camera to rapidly determine the location of the face in the frame and correct the other elements of the photo to produce a high-quality image.

For instance, if you photograph a companion peering through an aperture in a fort, the camera will likely focus on the fort. Face recognition focuses the camera on the face. It determines the optimal exposure based solely on the face.

What if a dozen children are peering out of the fort's numerous openings?

If they have snowballs, flee!

If not, the face recognition feature of your camera will likely capture all of them. Typically, face recognition works with up to 15 faces.

Face recognition has its limitations:

- Because it searches for a complete human visage with two eyes, it only works when the subject is facing forward and not in profile.

- Faces cannot be too distant.

- Faces must typically be perpendicular, i.e., the subject must be seated or standing and not reclined or lying down.

- Not effective with pets. Only supports human features.

- This mode requires subjects to be still, as it does not use a rapid shutter speed like sports mode.

- **How it operates:**

I have no idea! This is not one of the modes that could be duplicated manually. Wikipedia has an article on computer-based facial recognition science.

Preserving your camera:

- **Purifying the Lens**

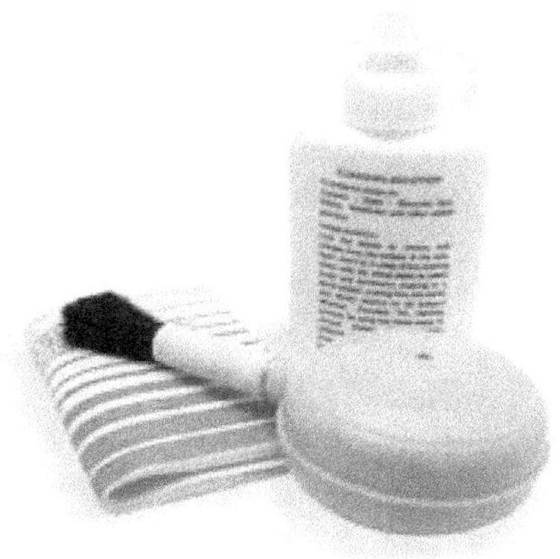

Occasionally, you'll need to sanitize the lens. Use a delicate watercolor brush or a lens blower brush to remove abrasive particulates that are loosely adhering.

Then, pour a couple drops of lens cleaning fluid directly onto a lens cloth or tissue and swab delicately in a circular motion. Take the lens to a camera store if a particulate is adhering to the lens.

- **Guard the Lens:**

It is advisable to keep the lens covered when not in use (some cameras do this automatically when powered down). This will result in Reduce the frequency with which it must be cleaned and preserve it when it is not in your possession.

- **Sun protection for your eyes and the camera's sensor:**

In the same way that it is unhealthy for your eyes to stare directly at the sun, it is unhealthy for your camera's sensor to have the lens pointed directly at the sun. Never gaze at the sun through a telescopic or telephoto lens, as this magnifies the intensity of the sun's beams.

- **Guard your camera against heat damage:**

Additionally, avoid leaving your camera in extremely heated environments, such as your automobile, in the summer. Between shots, keep it covered with a light-colored cloth when it is outside with you.

- **Prevent Degradation:**

Carry your camera in a padded or rigid camera case or a padded knapsack to protect it from impacts and abrasions.

- **Sand and sea do not mix well with cameras:**

Sand can cause significant damage to a camera. Not only can fine debris damage your lens, but it can also enter your camera and cause all sorts of issues. Here are some methods for safeguarding your camera:

- Remove sediment from the palms prior to taking up the camera.
- Consider carefully where you place your camera.
- Unprotected cameras are at high risk of damage during gusty conditions. Use a waterproof housing (which must be purchased separately) or leave your expensive camera at home and bring a disposable waterproof camera. A

Additionally, a waterproof camera captures excellent photographs when not submerged in water.

- Carry your camera in a dry container while on a boat, particularly when kayaking or river rafting! A camera in a dry case can be submerged in water without becoming damp. And waterproof containers levitate!

- **Rainfall photography:**

When taking photographs in the rain (as many professionals do), secure your camera with an umbrella or other means. Here are several methods for keeping your camera dry:

- Use a tripod with an umbrella attached (this will also keep you dry!).

- Utilize a device such as those reviewed on the website of Outdoor Photographer magazine.

- Bring a lens cleaning cloth and a small towel, and use them immediately if your camera becomes damp.

- Don't forget to keep your memory disks dry. If one gets damp, allow it to dry before using it so that your camera doesn't brief out!

- Transport your equipment in a watertight camera bag or knapsack.

- **Cold Weather: Preventing Condensation on Your Camera:**

Sledding, snowshoeing, and snowmen are all great photo opportunities. In addition to avoiding snowballs and storing your camera in its case when not in use, you should: not transport it from the cold directly into a heated space. You may have observed what happens to a chilly vessel when a less chilled beverage is poured into it. Alternatively, place a glass in the freezer for a few minutes then fill with water at ambient temperature. This is what happens when the lens is heated too quickly.

To prevent condensate from making your camera as moist as that glass, progressively rewarm it. One method is to remove the camera from the weather into a location with low humidity and slightly higher temperatures, such as the trunk of a vehicle parked in an unheated garage. If condensation renders your camera inoperable, transport it to a camera shop immediately. Place it in an impermeable bag with a basin of silica gel packets (these are sold in camera stores), secure the bag, and leave it for 48 to 72 hours. If the silica comes into contact with the camera, it can cause damage.

- **Camera Archiving:**

Regarding silica, if you are not going to use your camera for an extended period of time, remove the batteries and place a few silica gel sachets in the box to prevent injury from moisture. Place it in a dry environment. If you reside in or are traveling through a humid environment, always store your camera in a secure case when it is not in use.

- **Safeguarding the Data on Your Memory Cards:**

Similar to the video and cassette recordings of your parents' generation, the memory cards in your camera are susceptible to intense magnetic fields. One thing Even something as innocuous as a stereo speaker can obliterate the memory (your photographs) on the card. Additionally, to safeguard your photos before uploading them to your computer, Ensure that the camera has completed writing to the memory card prior to detaching it. Lastly, avoid mailing your memory cards. Some postal services, such as those in the United States, may use irradiation (for sanitizing), which can damage the semiconductors on credit cards. Now that we've covered the fundamentals, let's investigate some prominent photography genres and hone our abilities.

CHAPTER TWO

APPLICATIONS

Portraiture And Photojournalism

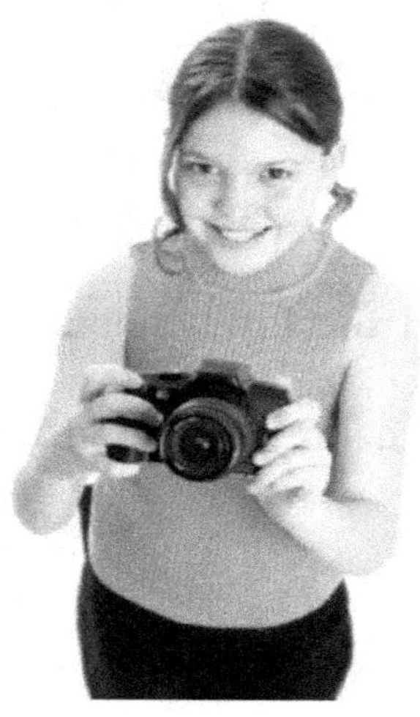

People are frequently the most difficult subjects to photograph, despite being the subject of the majority of the world's images. Consider a time when you were asked to pose with a group for a photo, and it took an eternity to get everyone to smile without making expressions or squinting at the same time. However, not all quality portraits of individuals must be so formal.

Some of your finest photos may be of your pals fooling off, a casual portrait of your parents on the front steps, or excellent street pictures.

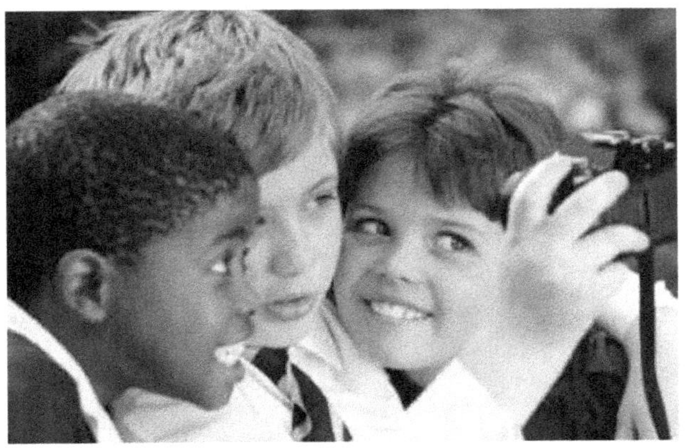

Portraiture:

What distinguishes a snapshot from a quality portrait? A photograph depicts a genuine likeness, but it is not uncommon for the subject to declare, "That doesn't look like me."

An expression or pose documented in a single moment does not always reflect the subject's typical expressions and methods of standing, reclining, etc. It is somewhat hit-or-miss. An excellent portrait reveals the subject's personality. How to obtain a portrait worthy of framing:

Set your camera's mode to portrait. Remember that this will automatically set the aperture wide so that the subject, and not the background, is in focus.

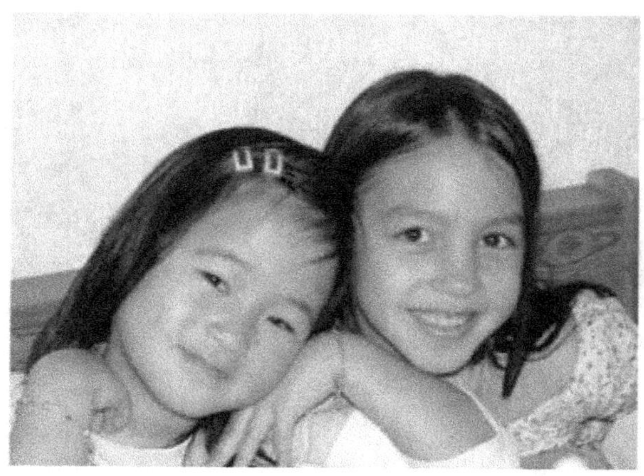

Background Check: No, not on your topic. Eliminate any debris. Remember that "clutter" in photography refers to anything that is not the subject of the photograph.

Excellent backdrops for portraits: Use your imagination, but here are some ideas: a plain wall (no cables or sockets visible), fabric draped on a wall or clothesline, bushes, a meadow, and the ocean. You can minimize or even obscure the background if it is at least 10 feet away from the subject.

Capturing a decent pose is essential. Since you have no film to fret about, take numerous photographs. Relax your subject through conversation, compliments, and lighthearted banter. Say "Hold that smile!" when you see a pose you like, and then film.

Zoom! You zoom so that your camera does not take wide-angle photographs. Wide-angle portraits, especially head-and-shoulders shots, frequently distort the subject, making them appear wider or more youthful. Here's how to proceed: Fill the frame, then take one step back and zoom to fill the frame again before shooting.

Props:

Individuality can be demonstrated through the use of personal objects. A prop could be a plush animal, a guitar, a baseball mitt, or anything else.

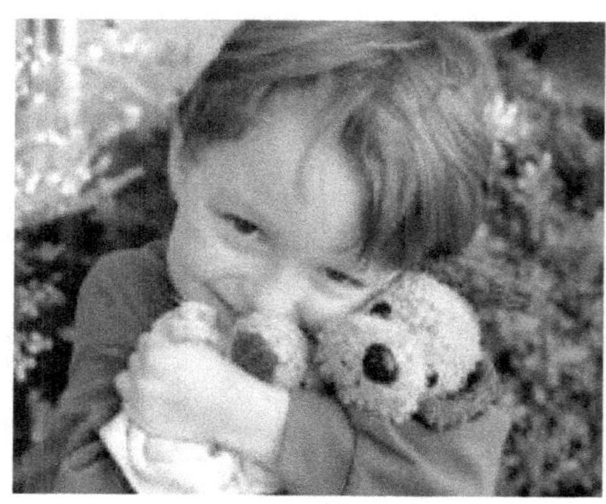

The lighting:

As with the majority of photographs, the optimal time and location for photographing people is typically outdoors during the golden hours when the light is gentle. Under a cloudy atmosphere, there is a second viable option. Use fill illumination when shadows from the sun are a problem. The finest indoor lighting source is natural light. If window light is too intense, mitigate it with a light fabric. When purchasing new light bulbs, choose a full-spectrum bulb that is as close as possible to natural light. Low ceiling lighting creates dreadful shadows, so avoid shooting there. Full-spectrum lighting is second only to natural light. Alternatively, adjust the white balance in your image editor if this option is not available on your camera. If you do not use the camera's flash, red-eye is typically avoided.

Activate the red-eye reduction feature on your camera if you must use it. If that doesn't work, try using a photo editor to remove the object. Have a good time! Remember to joke around and offer sincere compliments (as the professionals do) if your subject is camera shy. You could also allow him to select his preferences.

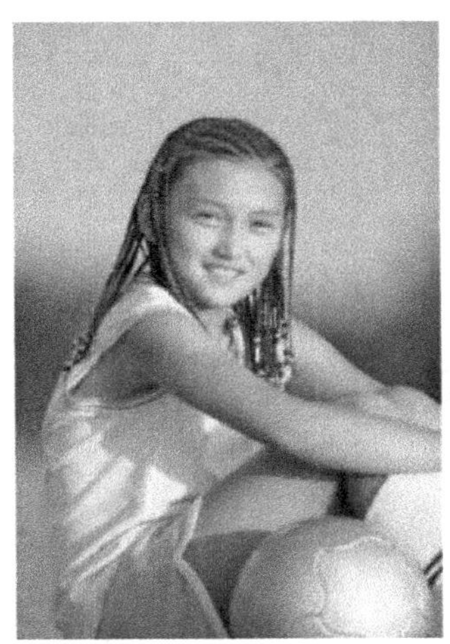

Family Portraits:

Instead of the typical group photo in which everyone is lined up shoulder to shoulder like a police lineup, group subjects together in more visually appealing and fascinating formations.

By stacking them on stairs, boulders, and other objects, you can add height and depth to your image. Create an intimate appearance by placing everyone's heads close together. To add depth, have subjects incline or pivot slightly toward the camera.

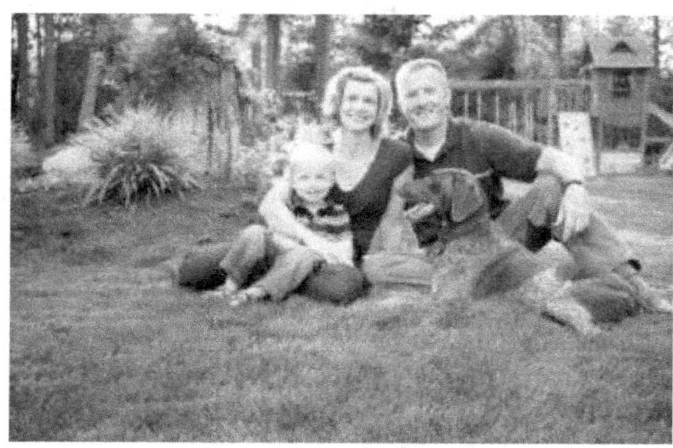

Specify relationships. A sibling and sister could have their arms around each other's shoulders, for instance.

Allow everyone to unwind prior to beginning the photograph. Take multiple photographs in case someone blinks, a sibling nudges his sister, etc.

Regarding grins, avoid freezing them for more than a few seconds, or you'll get unnatural expressions. The moment you give the signal, everyone grins and fires!

To include yourself in a photograph, use a remote shutter release or the camera's timer, if available.

Concerts, recitals, and other low-light environments:

Suppose you want to photograph your friend's first ballet recital, but the digital camera's light meter warns there is not enough light to accurately expose the scene, and signs on the walls prohibit the use of flash. If your camera's ISO is adjustable, try a higher setting. Or set your camera to "ISO Auto" to have it automatically select a higher ISO.

As you may recall from Part 1, increasing the ISO beyond 100 on the majority of point-and-shoot cameras can result in digital noise (small colored specks in the image). Numerous people use noise removal software, such as Noise Ninja, to fantastic effect.

Urban Photography:

Street photography is a form of documentary photography in which subjects are captured in candid public settings.

Local newspapers, National Geographic, and travel guides provide examples. This will come in handy while on vacation.

Places where people are accustomed to being in close proximity, such as congested cities, carnivals, parades, outdoor concerts, and community events, are ideal for taking these types of photographs. There are instances, however, when it is inappropriate to approach someone and aim your camera at them, such as when they are peacefully reading on a park bench.

While in the United States and some other nations it is not required by law to ask permission before photographing someone, it is considered courteous to do so. There are numerous methods to accomplish this. One method is to smile, aim your camera at them, elevate your eyebrows, and wait for an affirmation or frown. It is best to respect someone's privacy if they shake their head "no" or otherwise object. However, if the individual is performing in a sporting event, parade, etc., or if you are photographing a large group, requesting permission is not anticipated. Always obtain parental consent before photographing another child. Obviously, you must practice caution and avoid approaching strangers without parental supervision.

Sometimes a sign or object will lend humor or significance to a photograph.

This child appears to be in conflict with his sandwich. Please take note of the sign in the upper left corner.

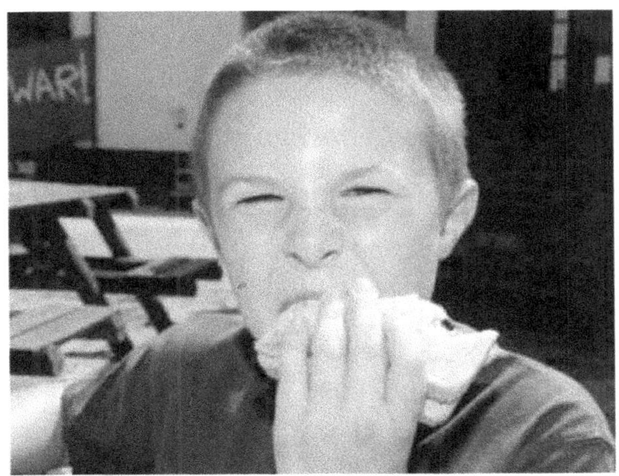

While it is lawful to photograph individuals in public without their permission, there are numerous restrictions on how these images may be used.

For instance, written permission is required for commercial use but not editorial use. Your publication is editorial. Advertising and websites that sell or promote products are commercial. Private property is subject to the same laws.

Legal handbooks, such as the Legal Handbook for Photographers: The Rights and Liabilities of Making Images, are available in their entirety if you ever become interested in selling photographs of individuals.

Technical Advice:

In the genuine sense of photojournalism, you are using an image to convey a narrative. In contrast to the majority of photographs, include as much context as possible.

To obtain the background, use landscape orientation. Utilize athletic mode to halt action.

Manual controls allow for greater creativity, but these two modes will suffice for the time being. Use portrait mode to fill the frame with a subject that is relatively near.

Holiday Lights

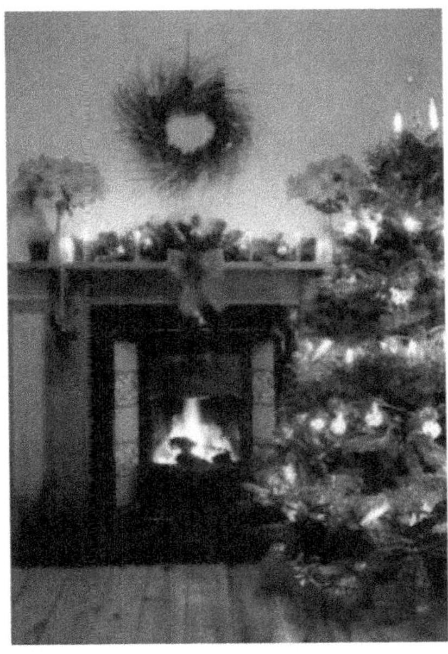

Numerous special occasions and holidays, including Christmas, Hanukkah, birthdays, Halloween, New Year's Eve, and the Fourth of July, feature candles and/or festive lighting. Ofttimes, turning off your camera's flash is the easiest method to capture holiday lighting.

Flash: On or Off?

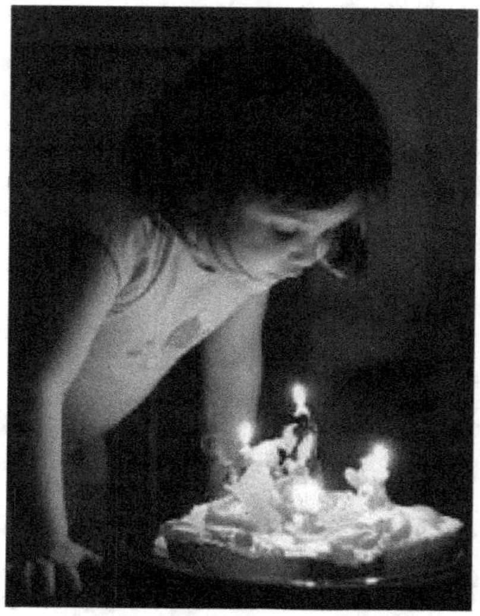

Typically, holiday decorations and candles photograph best without additional lighting. When photographing Christmas trees, holiday lighting, and candles, you should turn off your flash and shoot in automatic mode.

As with most photography "rules," there are exceptions to this rule.

For example, select the night portrait setting when photographing a person in front of a light display.

Lastly, shoot at dusk for a beautiful dark blue sky, as seen in so many magazine images of holiday lighting.

Make a Desire:

A birthday candle ceremony can be difficult to photograph. But once you have it, beware: you will eternally be the designated birthday photographer on your block.

Most people make the error of attempting to capture both the candles and a well-lit image of the person's visage. Instead, do the following...

Take a picture of the birthday individual with the cake (perhaps while the birthday wish is being considered). Utilize a night portrait. Set the shutter speed to 1/30 if your camera lacks aperture priority but has shutter speed priority. This will capture both the subject and the lighting.

Then, transition to portrait mode with light to capture the individual extinguishing the candles.

Extra Candle Advice:

To create stunning photographs with people and candles, such as a birthday cake candle ceremony, the lighting of the final candle on the Menorah, or loved ones in front of a lit Christmas tree, attempt the following:

Disable the flare. Place an incandescent light so that it illuminates the person without competing with the other lights or candles.

The use of fireworks:

Establish a position with an unobstructed view of where the pyrotechnics will explode. Be cautious of obstructions such as utility lines. If an obstruction cannot be averted, you can likely remove it using your photo editor.

If the fireworks display is taking place over water, do not take pictures from a bridge. Passing vehicles can cause sufficient vibration to obscure your photographs. Similar reasoning apply to avoiding bleachers.

These are more difficult. You can photograph pyrotechnics in default mode, but if your camera supports one of the following settings, you can capture their brilliance and flaming trails. Set your camera's mode to pyrotechnics. Or, set your camera's mode to landscape. (Or, if manual focus is available, set it to infinity.) Set your shutter speed just long enough to capture the entire scene, but not so long that smoke is captured.

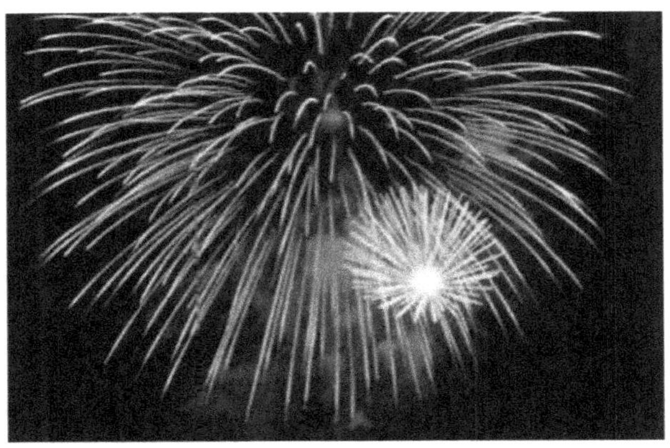

The optimal shutter speed is typically around 3 seconds. Longer is also advantageous if there is no odor. Additionally, disable the preset white balance (the pyrotechnics mode does this automatically). Otherwise, your camera will dull the colors and vibrancy. Use a sturdy camera support in either case to prevent distortion caused by minor camera movements when using a delayed shutter speed.

On your cue, aim, and fire! If the display begins before it is entirely dark, you will be able to photograph the sunset or twilight sky alongside the first pyrotechnics. You will also be able to capture objects, such as vessels on a lake, that you would not typically see in a night photo.

Since you will not be using your light, swivel around to capture people's reactions during a pyrotechnics display. Later, you can display these alongside your photos of pyrotechnics.

Halloween Evening Lighting:

Use night portrait mode when photographing in your neighborhood to capture your trick-or-treating companions with Halloween lighting or Jack-o'-lanterns in the background.

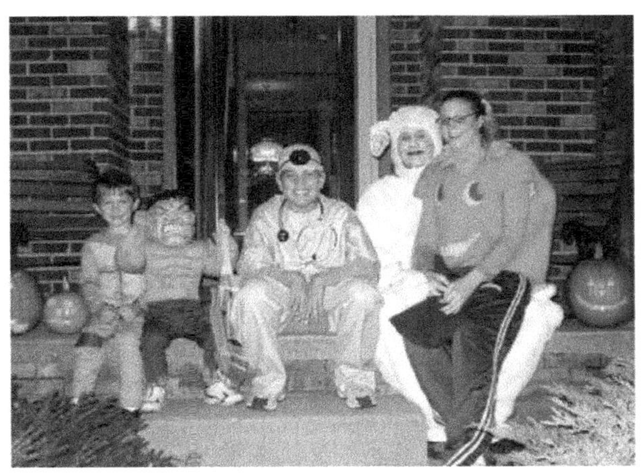

Here are a few more suggestions:

Try out this spooky illumination technique when photographing ghosts and princesses on Halloween night. This will create uncanny facial shadows. Consider this for Halloween portraits.

Turn off the light if you want to take excellent photos of Jack-o'-lanterns.

Remember to complete the frame with a single or multiple pumpkins.

Sports Photography

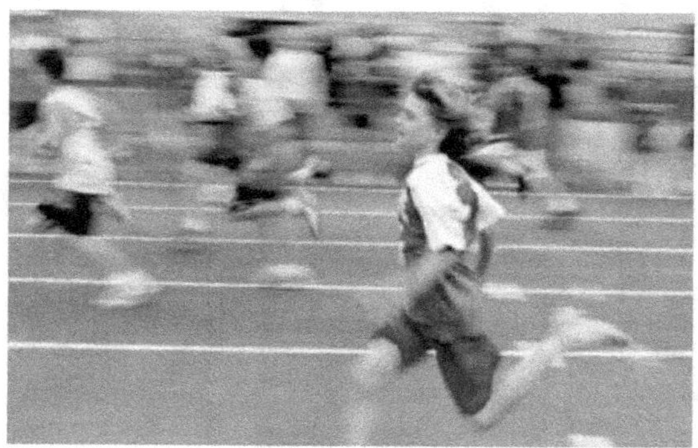

Learning how to take excellent sports photographs enables you to capture extremely interesting images of your friends and family. It is not sufficient to simply photograph the action. Look for facial expressions and zoom in on faces to capture their resolve, effort, and success.

Sports photography is not restricted to soccer and track and field events. In addition to conventional athletics, there is skateboarding, martial arts, BMX, etc.

Sport photography presents numerous challenges and rewards. The athletes will appreciate the photographs you take of them and their peers.

Are you all set? Here is the strategy.

Get the scoop:

The most important aspect of sports photography is knowing when and where the action will occur so you can be ready to capture it. Therefore, having a fundamental comprehension of the sport is extremely beneficial (Wikipedia is a great resource for this). Thus, you will know where to position your camera, what types of images to attempt to capture, and where the most thrilling plays are likely to occur.

Exercise your skills:

Focus:

If the autofocus on your camera is so sluggish that you're missing photos, try this: Concentrate on the chest region surrounding the numerals or team name. Autofocus is more responsive to contrast. Be prepared to capture faces, the ball, action, and contact for the most compelling action photos. The greater the number of these elements captured in a single image, the better.

Freeze out:

In sports mode, your camera will choose a rapid shutter speed and capture the action.

Or Blur:

Have you ever noticed that in some of the best sports photographs, the action is distinct while the background is blurry? It draws attention to the action while placing the background in the background.

Photographers accomplish this by diminishing the depth of field. It is also possible if your camera has aperture priority. You only need to reduce the f-stop value. The smaller the f-stop value, the less background is captured.

In this case, you would increase the depth of field by increasing the f-number.

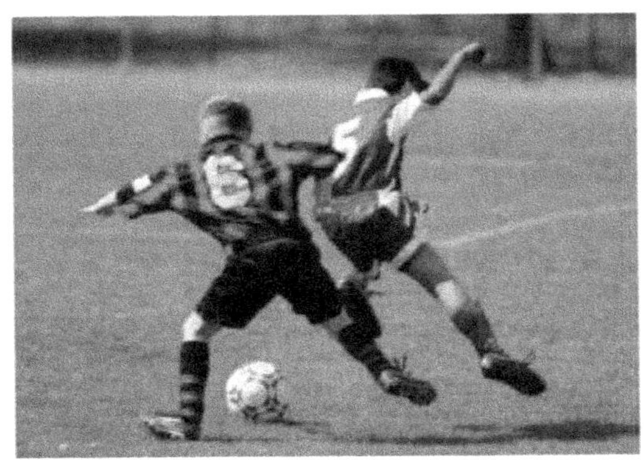

Pan:

If the sport is played indoors, the light may be too dim to use a rapid shutter speed or sports mode. You can pan your camera in automatic mode to capture action. Additionally, panning blurs the background (as seen in the image at the beginning of this chapter). This effect is utilized by many professionals because it conveys the sensation of movement and brings the image to life. Due to the fact that panning only functions from right to left and left to right, you cannot use it for all game action.

This is how: Firmly plant your feet on the earth. Before taking a photograph, follow your subject with your camera, using only the upper portion of your body. Before the action ramps up, begin tapping the shutter button while following the subject until it closes.

For instance, if you are photographing a track meet, observe the approaching racers through the viewfinder. Then, point the camera at the runner's torso that you wish to photograph. Press the shutter release button and follow the racer while keeping the camera pointed at the racer's torso.

In other words, the subject must remain stationary within the frame as you adjust the camera. If you hadn't panned the camera, the racer would appear as a large haze. However, because you moved the camera at the same speed as the subject, you captured a distinct image.

It requires practice, but when done correctly, only the subject (or a significant portion of the subject) will be in focus, while everything else will be blurred by motion. Quite interesting.

More Advice:

If feasible, leave the bleachers and move closer to the action. By employing magnification (remember, optical, not digital) from the sidelines, it is possible to produce a more engaging image than from the terraces. You can also identify angles that will minimize peripheral distractions.

Don't fret if you're trapped in the bleachers. You can obtain some excellent perspectives from various stand heights and by using your magnification.

The features of athletes or a small portion of the action have been captured in some of the finest sports photographs ever taken. But don't belittle your abilities if you can't produce professional-quality photographs. Just look at those gigantic telephoto lenses. Having an SLR also helps.

On the other hand, point-and-shoot cameras are extremely versatile. Even professionals, including sports photographers, occasionally use point-and-shoot cameras!

Pet Photography

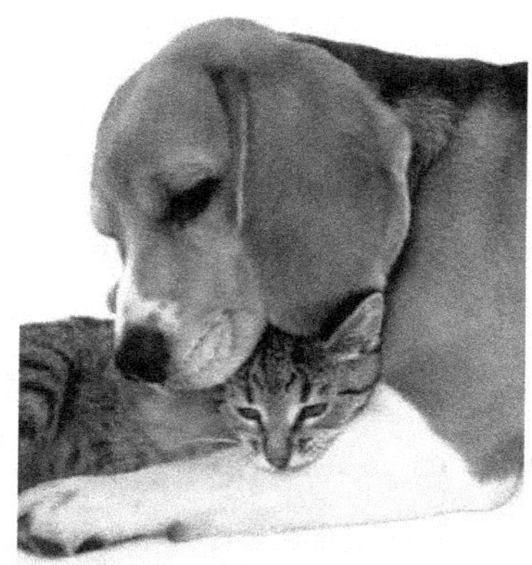

Observing Motion:

We'd never miss a perfect picture if our canines knew how to play freeze tag. Sports mode is frequently the optimal option for photographing canines, cats, parrots, hamsters, and virtually every other type of creature imaginable.

Burst mode is also useful, particularly when your pet is playing or otherwise energetic.

Sometimes it's enjoyable to obscure the motion. The example of a dog pursuing its tail comes to mind. Choose a mode with a reduced shutter speed, such as portrait, to obscure motion. Or, if your companion is running in a relatively straight line, try panning, as these two friends are doing. Remember to effortlessly adjust your camera.

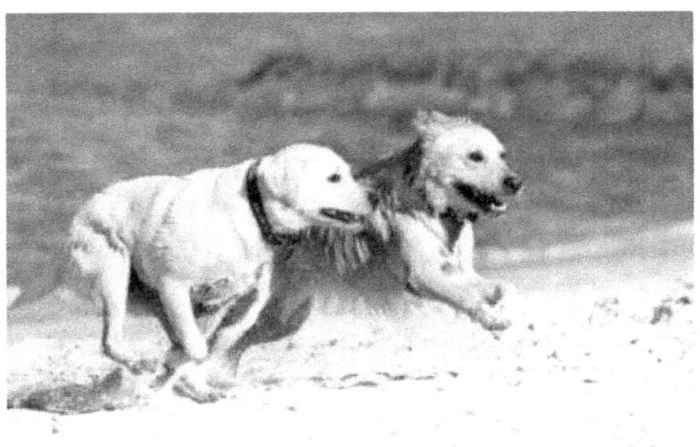

Light:

As always, natural light is preferable. Pets are more sensitive to light than humans. If you must use a light, keep it at least four feet away from your pet's face, or consult your camera's manual for recommended distances.

As in most situations, the golden hours are ideal for photographing canines outdoors (see the chapter on light). Sidelights add shadows to overcome a bland appearance. If your companion has a delicate pelt, cloudy weather is ideal.

With one exception, overcast weather is beneficial for most pets. Bright sunlight can accentuate the color and texture of your pet's black coat.

Identifying Personality:

What distinguishes your companion from others of the same species that you have observed, besides the fact that he or she is the finest animal on the planet? Consider its eccentric behavior and unique personality.

Now, choose a time of day when the illumination is optimal and you have the greatest chance of capturing your companion doing its thing. As is typical when photographing canines, set your camera to the sports or action mode.

Whether you are outside with a dog, cat, horse, or other animal, be prepared to invest some time. Follow your companion around slowly and silently while maintaining a safe distance (remember to magnify!). This will allow you to obtain the most candid photos. Prepare to focus and fire.

If you want your companion to liven up and run towards you and your camera, try making a few very subtle sounds or tossing something in the desired direction.

Including a person or object that is special to your companion is another way to demonstrate personality and context.

What is your position:

Also keep in mind that, similar to your human friends and family, canines appear differently from different angles. Therefore, attempt framing using various methods. Get close-ups, medium shots, and full-body images.

Most individuals take photographs of their dogs from above. And in most circumstances, this results in dull images. Get down to the level of your pet's eyes, whether by squatting or reclining on the ground.

Sometimes it's a good idea to take a photo from above, such as when your companion is gazing up at you with an endearing expression.

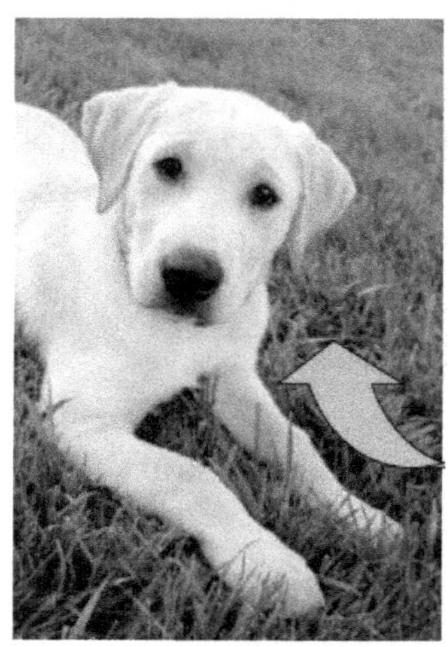

Consider the eyes:

The irises of canines, cats, and horses are extremely expressive. This is one reason to concentrate on them. Additionally, unless you intend to concentrate on the eyes, you may wind up focusing on the tip of your pet's snout, resulting in slightly out-of-focus eyes. This is also a great concept for spontaneous photos.

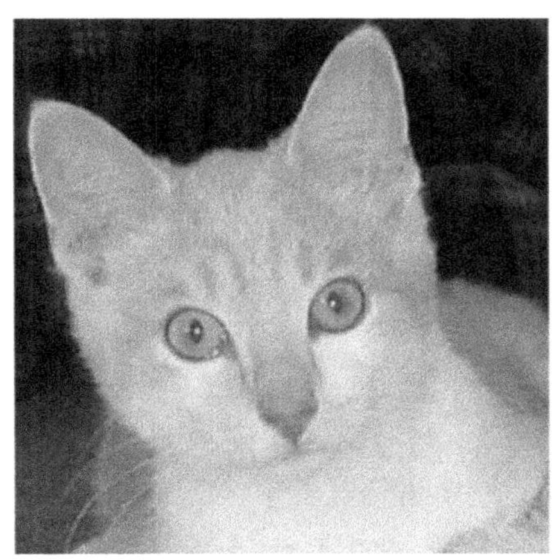

The Background:

Look for backgrounds with contrast that complement but do not detract, like a green hedge for a yellow lab. Zoom in if the background is distracting. Typically, this will obscure the background.

Grooming:

The camera captures details that we would normally overlook, such as mucus in the corner of an eye, shedding fur, and a random object trapped in the fur. Therefore, prior to photographing your companion, prepare a tissue and brush.

Landscape Photography

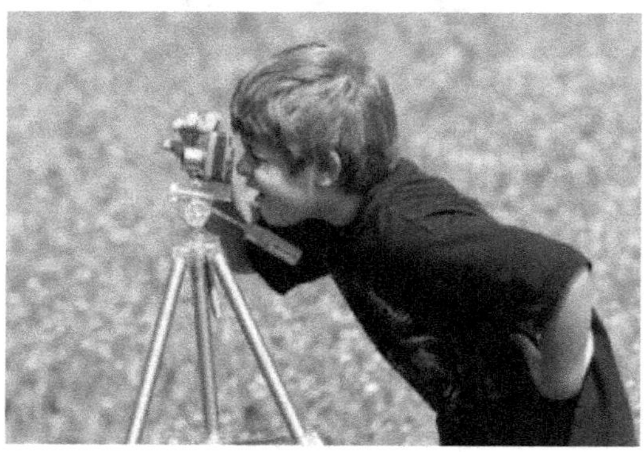

When you go on family vacations, do you enjoy looking at the scenery? Do you like to just sit and gaze at a nice view?

If yes, then you will probably enjoy landscape photography. If not, then taking pictures of sunsets, mountains and seascapes might bore you. The nice thing about photography is there's something for everyone – portraits, candid shots of people, sports, pets, wildlife, and lots more.

One of America's most famous photographers, Ansel Adams, is best known for his landscape photographs, such as The Tetons and Snake River, picture to the left.

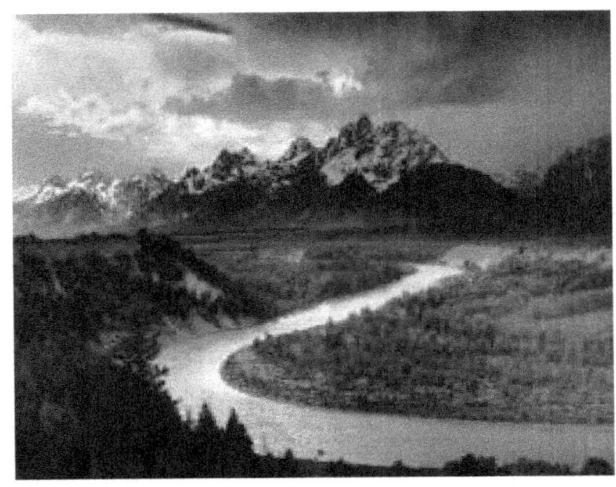

What exactly is Landscape Photography:

It depend on whom you ask... This is often defined as a picture of a natural scene. People, if in the photograph, are generally a very small part of the pictures and used for a sense of scale. Many landscape photographers also include cityscapes or urban landscapes as a type of landscape photography while others draw the line between natural and urban.

Lighting for Landscapes :

The key to three-dimensional looking landscapes, ones that really pop, is the quality of the light.

- The golden hours can almost always be counted on for nice soft lighting, but we won't stop there.

- Under overcast skies, color intensifies while highlights are subdued.

- Clouds cast dramatic shadows.

- Contrast, such as between bright, autumn leaves and a strong blue sky creates drama and often enhances the graphic quality of an image.

- Fog softens a scene.

And then there are the sunrises and sunsets, but first let's take a look at some of the basics for composing the type of landscape photography that you can be proud to hang on walls and enter into competitions.

Landscape Composition Tips:

- **Foreground:**

Frame your picture so that a point of interest is in the foreground. This draws the viewer into the image and adds a sense of depth. The

point of interest could be a boulder, tree, person, animal...just about
anything.

- **Horizons:**

Compose your picture so that the horizon appears straight.

If the sky is dramatic, showcase it by placing the horizon on the
upper two thirds of your shot. If it's the foreground that holds more
interest, fill only the top third of the frame with sky.

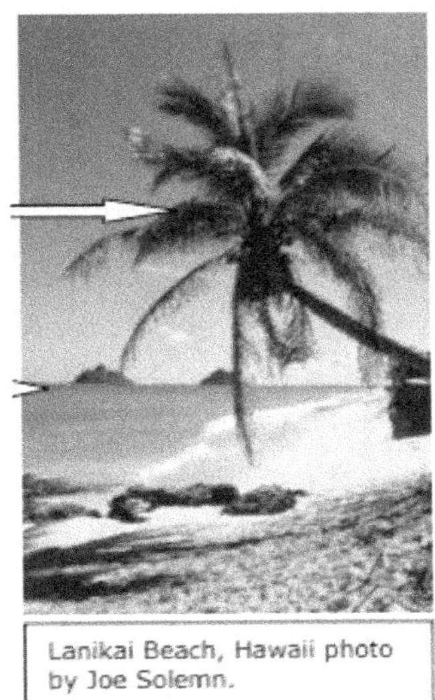

Lanikai Beach, Hawaii photo by Joe Solemn.

- **Lines:**

A road, river, fence or other line in the image directs attention into
your picture. When your scene has a line like one of these, select a

spot or an angle where major lines in the scene lead your eye toward the main center of interest.

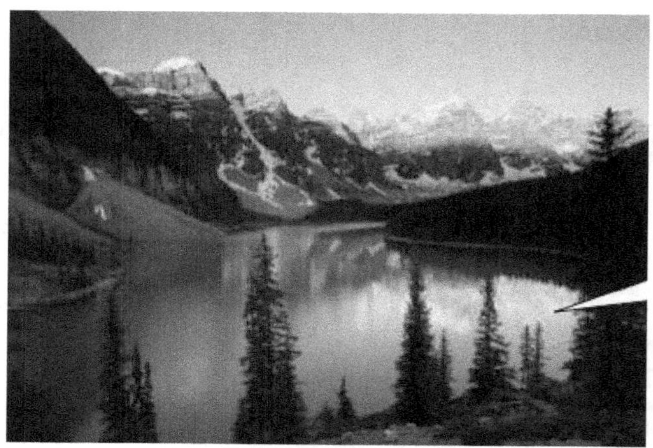

- **Focal Points:**

A landscape photograph without a focal point can look empty and leave your viewer's eyes with no place to rest. A focal point can be a structure, tree, rock formation, boulder, silhouette, etc. One of the most pleasing ways to place your focal point in the frame is to use the Rule of Thirds.

- **Depth of Field:**

This is where compact cameras are at their best. They have much better depth of field than SLRs. If your camera is set to landscape mode, it will have a large depth of field, bringing as much as possible into focus.

- **Scale:**

The cliff may not look all that big in a photo—until you put it into perspective. For example, including a boat beneath the cliff will provide the kind of scale that brings the "Wow" factor to the towering cliff.

- **Simplify:**

As always avoid clutter. In the case of landscape photography, this clutter may come in the way of a telephone wire, an airplane overhead or trash on the ground. Remember, you may be able to clean up the clutter with a good photo editor, but if you can avoid it and still get the shot, all the better.

- **Find an Angle:**

Look around for points of view. Try various spots at a scenic look out.

Sunsets:

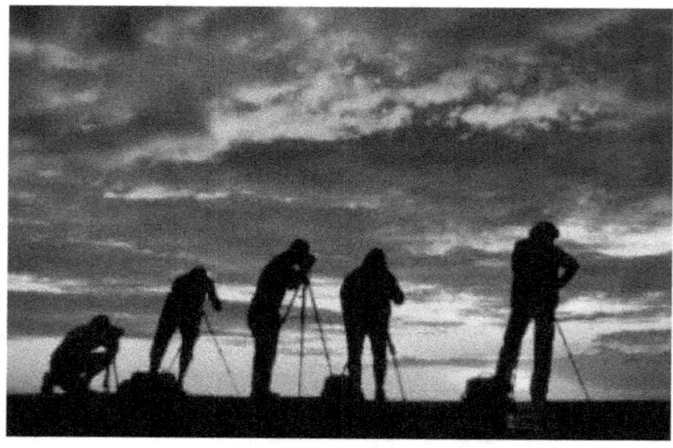

Everyone seems to love sunset photos. To make yours stand out, follow these tips:

You'll often find the most majestic sunsets over large masses of water because humidity with the hot sun produces dramatic clouds.

An unobstructed view of the sun setting on the horizon is also a big plus.

When composing your shot, use the landscape composition tips. During a sunset the point of interest in the foreground (person, tree, etc.) will be in silhouetted by the backlight from the sun. This adds a nice touch.

If a person is in the foreground and it's someone you know ask him or her to do different poses, like the kind you see in magazines: yoga positions, reaching hands up to the heavens, holding a surfboard...

Camera Settings for Sunsets:

Dramatic sunsets are made up of yellows, oranges, blues, and even magentas. This is a good thing, but your camera's automatic white balance doesn't think so. It compares to what is normal, not knowing this is a sunset. This means the auto white balance will cause the camera to compensate for the brilliant and saturated colors by dulling them down.

So if you can, turn off the auto white balance and set it to the warm side. If your camera has a color lens selection, try some shots with the red filter selected. Professionals do this frequently so that the camera captures the brilliance that otherwise it might miss.

Or if your camera doesn't offer these features, use sunset mode. This works for sunrises too. It automatically sets the best focus and exposure (no flash). The white balance will be set to daylight to capture and keep the warm shift in color balance.

- **Caution:**

In the excitement of the moment don't forget It is dangerous to your eyes to look directly at the shining yellow sun. It can also damage your camera's sensor. Don't look directly at it until it is low enough in the sky to have turned a dark red. If you're using a long lens or zoom, this is even more dangerous because the sun's intensity is magnified.

Winter Wonderlands:

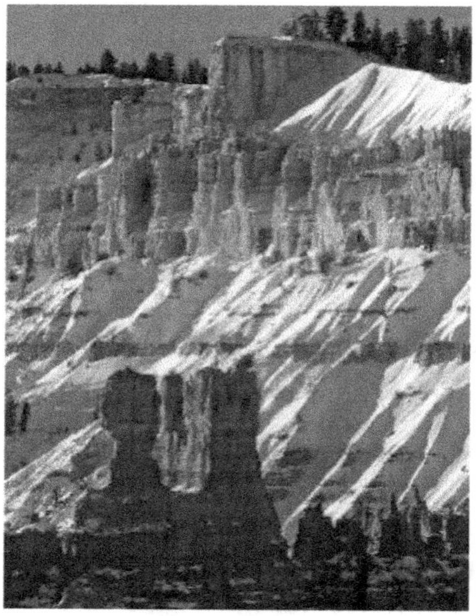

Snowy landscapes can make beautiful photos, but there are a few tricks to the lighting. The camera in its attempt to white balance often adds a blue or gray tint to the snow. The best mode for preventing this is snow mode (who would have guessed). The second best mode is beach mode.

Or if you can, turn off automatic white balance, set it manually to the warmer side and shoot in landscape mode.

Blue can be good though, depending on the effect your after. And when it is contrasted (such as with the sunlit, red rocks on left), the contrast adds to the drama and beauty However, when everything is blanketed in white, try composing your frame with a single colored object, such as a cardinal perched on a fence post or a sled.

For falling snow, use the flash to fix the movement of the snowflakes. This will improve images that could otherwise look dull or blurred.

Shoot during the golden hours, when the sun is low on the horizon, to capture the texture and shape of the snow on what would otherwise look like a uniform field of white.

When shooting out in the cold, remember before you go back inside, to protect your camera from condensation.

Urban Landscapes:

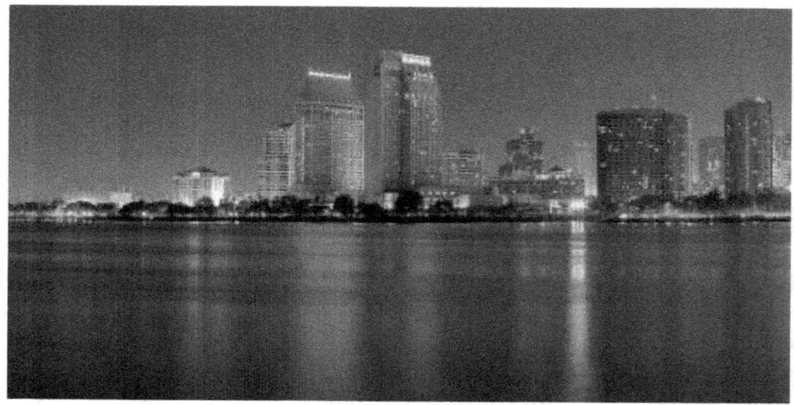

Also called cityscapes, these are often photographed at night. Be sure turn off your flash off so that lights aren't dulled by it.

Another favorite time of the day for cityscape photographers is early in the morning and not just because this golden hour diffused the light. You'll also likely have cleaner streets and less people. One person or a few is fine for scale, but you want the focus on the structures, or if it's interesting, the sky.

To learn more about landscape photography and view some amazing photographs, check out the online, free Outdoor Photographer magazine.

Vacation Images

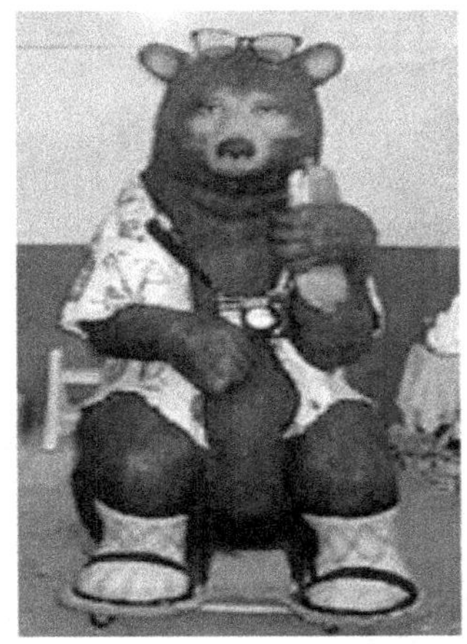

I've reserved this for last because vacation or travel photography is one area of photography. where practically every talent and technique taught in this book can be applied.

Consider that vacation and travel photographs always include people, landscapes, and frequently flora, animals (in zoos, aquariums, or the untamed), nocturnal pictures, and even occasionally pets.

Tips for Taking Better Vacation Photos:

Scale up for drama:

Not all life's drama is unpleasant. Making your photographs more dramatic increases their visual appeal and interest. One way to add drama is by demonstrating magnitude. You can do this by adding people or natural elements to your photographs of large objects such as monuments, the world's largest redwood, and the tallest building. natural environments.

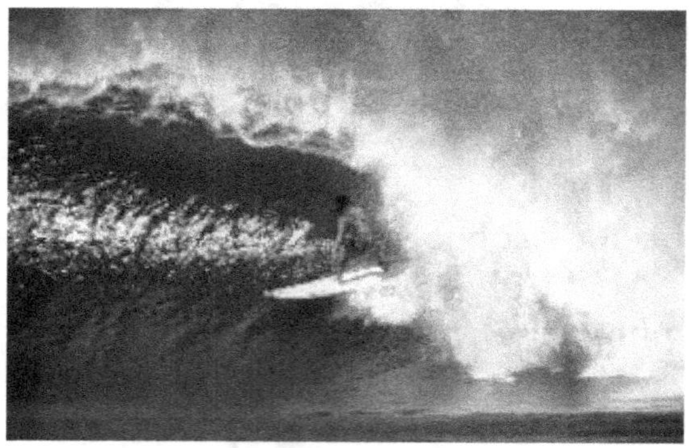

Be wary of clutter:

In the euphoria of seeing so many photographic opportunities, it's easy to lose focus regarding the backdrop. Relocating a few feet could help eliminate debris such as power lines, billboards, and individuals strolling through your image.

Take images of the locals:

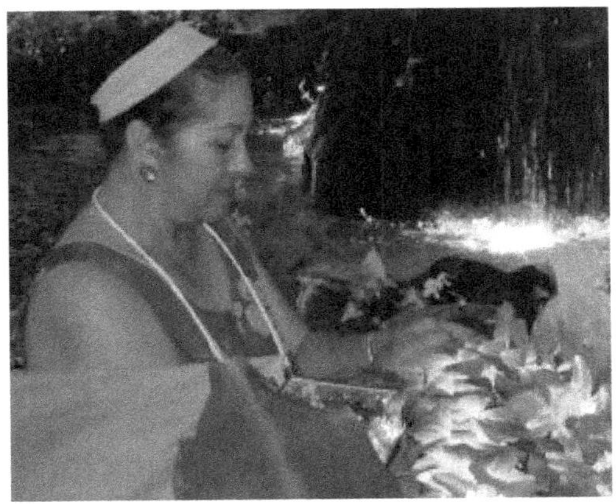

Request your guardians' assistance engage in conversation with the locals. You will Educate yourself on their culture and improve your photography by storing information you may have missed out on.

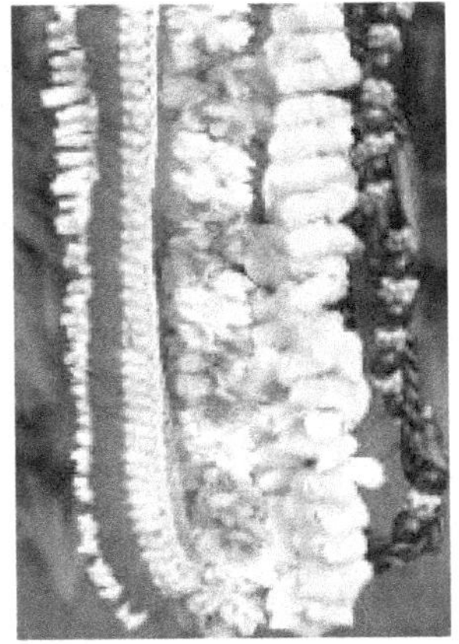

Learn how to express "May I take your picture, please?" in languages spoken throughout the world. where you will be traveling. Offer to send a copy to those you photograph. Carry a notebook and a pen pencil for noting names, addresses, and email addresses. You could earn some pleasant correspondence with friends with other children.

Take numerous photographs of individuals engaging in activities, including your family and the locals. But Don't pose with strangers.

If you don't ask them to smile, mules don't mind posing; however, if you ask them to smile, they may object.

Candid & Unique:

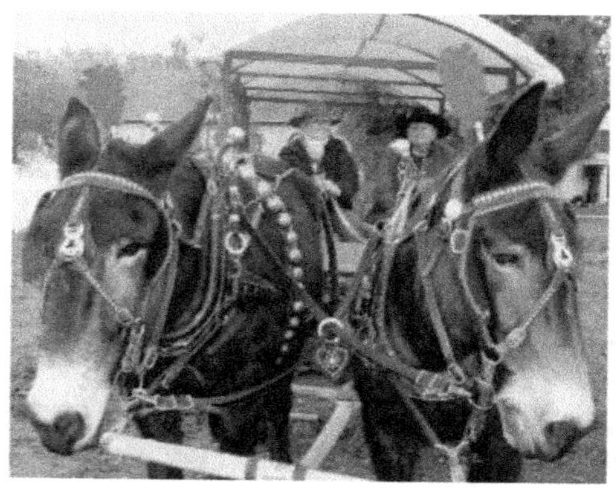

The finest travel photographs are candid, but almost every vacation album also includes portraits of the family in front of breathtaking vistas and renowned landmarks. Use the camera's self-timer to include yourself in the photo.

Photograph what interests you, not what you believe should interest you because it is featured on postcards in every store. You can always add postcards to your collection of vacation mementos. Unique subjects make for excellent images. Keep an eye out for the unusual and photograph it if you encounter it.

Providing an Account of Your Trip:

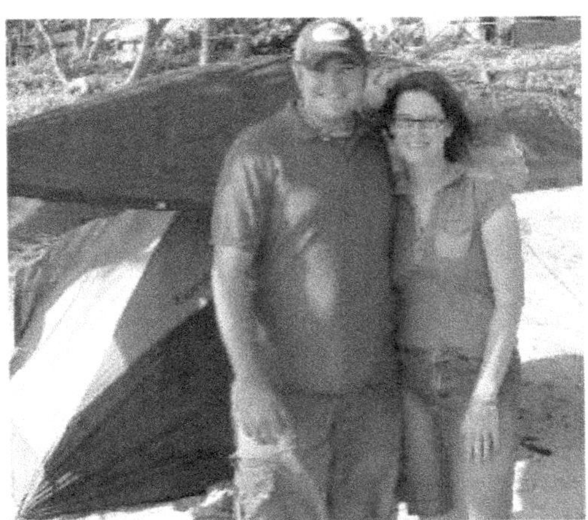

You may wish to use your photographs to convey the story of your travel from departure to return. Include highlights such as your campground neighbors, an unusual meal you had, activities, and the expression on your sister's face when she saw (fill in the blank) for the first time. This can make a wonderful family album, but with annotations, it could also serve as a photo essay for school.

You and your parents may have viewed fascinating travelogues in the form of slide presentations on YouTube. Using your photo editor and a little practice, you can also create these. An online family album is an alternative option.

Make audio or written notes on your camera or in a notebook so that you can subsequently add captions to your photos.

Camera Operations:

If you will be near or in the water, bring disposable waterproof cameras.

Remember that even for the most seasoned professionals, not every photograph will be worth keeping. Taking multiple photographs will provide you with more options for viewing on your computer at home. Unless you have a means to submit your photos while on vacation, such as a laptop, you should carry spare memory cards. Finally, prepare your camera for the following day by recharging the batteries and replacing the memory card each evening. In this manner, you will be set to go in the morning! And when you return, you'll have a large number of incredible photographs to upload to your computer.

CHAPTER THREE

THE DIGITAL DARKROOM

Uploading and Organizing

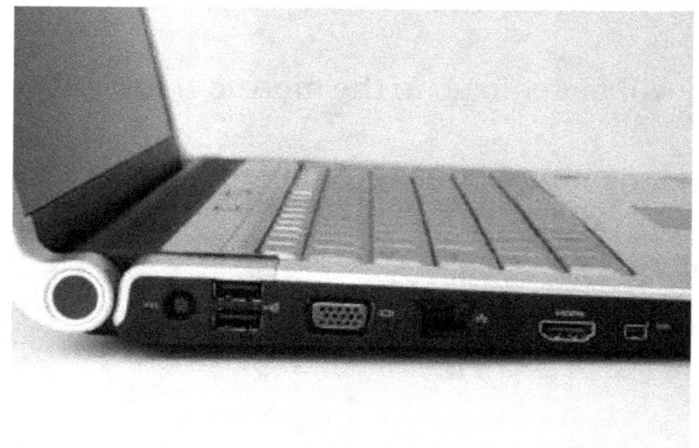

Create files for your photographs to become more organized:

When you transfer photos from a memory card to your computer, they are automatically saved in the folder designated for pictures. On Windows computers, this is the "My Pictures" folder within "My Documents." On Macs, this is the "Pictures" subdirectory in the personal directory. This is acceptable for an occasional photographer.

However, you will likely amass a large number of images quickly, and storing them all in a single folder can be problematic. Here is one method to organize them:

Review your images on the LCD of your camera during playback. Consider the different categories you possess. Write them down. You may have a family, pets, a vacation, friends, a soccer team, etc.

Now, open your default images folder and create a subfolder for each of these subjects inside.

- **Optional:**

You might want to include the date at the beginning of each folder's name. The year should be entered first, followed by the month and date. I do this because, by default, the computer's operating system arranges folders alphabetically by name. Adding the date causes it to also arrange them chronologically.

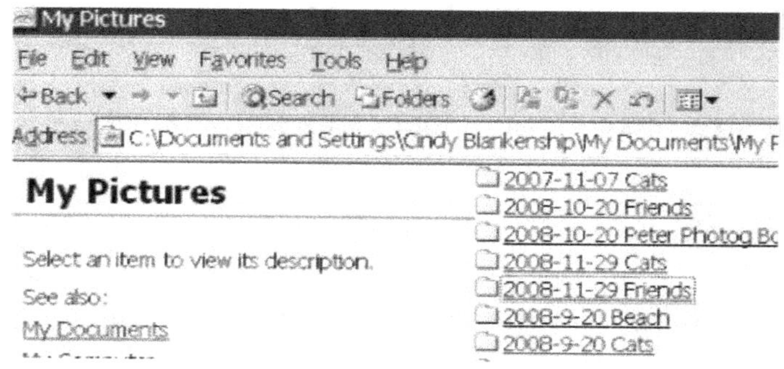

This eliminates the need to name each photo individually, as you can view their thumbnails rapidly enough to determine what you have, as there are fewer photos in each folder.

Some who do not have a large number of photos in the same category prefer to omit the year. Others give each container a unique, descriptive name, such as "friends goofing off." The more photos you take, the more time and effort you will need to invest in organizing them.

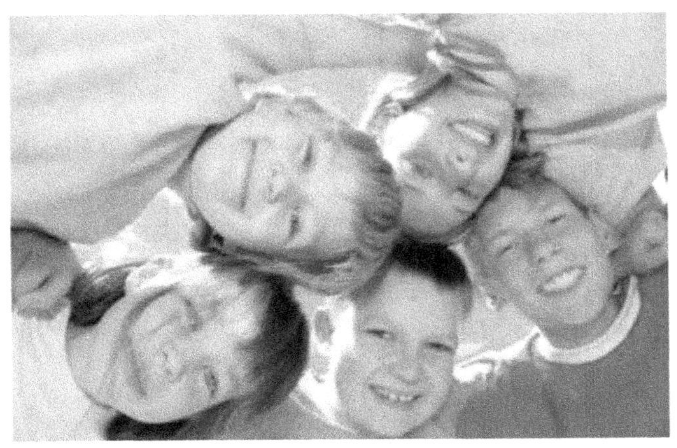

Before you copy the next group of photos to your computer, repeat this process: peruse your photographs, note the primary subjects or events, and create folders for them, starting with the dates. If you do not create new folders with dates, you will add new photos to the existing subfolders. Then, only new subfolders for new categories would be created. This means that you may wind up with a large number of images in one subfolder. If you do it this way, it's a good idea to name each photo, as there may be too many for fast thumbnail views.

Now that the folders for your photos have been created, it is time to upload them to your computer.

Attaching your camera to your computer:

Consult the manual for your camera for specific connection instructions, and adhere to them. Charge your camera's battery or connect it to a power adapter so you don't lose any photos during this procedure.

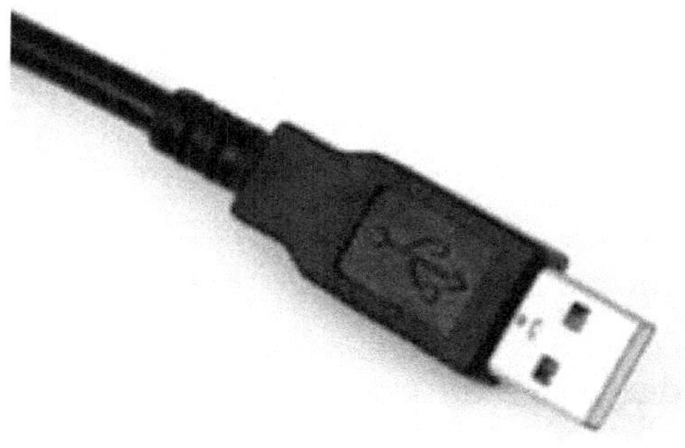

Start with the computer powered on and the camera turned off. Then, one end of the cable is connected to a USB interface on the computer, while the other end is connected to the camera.

Once the connections are secure, switch on the camera and set it to transfer mode (or follow the instructions on your playback device).

The images on the memory card of your camera will be automatically copied to the preset picture folder ("My Pictures" or "Pictures").

It may prompt you to delete the images from your memory card. If you are naming each photo rather than simply using the file number, you may delete them.

If you are using file numbers as file identifiers, eliminate them from the camera's memory card, not the computer. This is because reformatting on a computer resets the file number, resulting in identical file numbers for multiple images.

However, another reason to discard photos from the camera later is so that you have time to create backups.

Before deactivating your camera, you must ensure that it is no longer in transfer mode. Once you receive the signal indicating that the transfer has been completed, you may power off your camera.

Now, you have a few tasks remaining.

Do you recall the folders you created? It's time to transfer the photographs to them. If you open the folders, you can easily drag and drop photos into them using the thumbnail view.

Always have a backup:

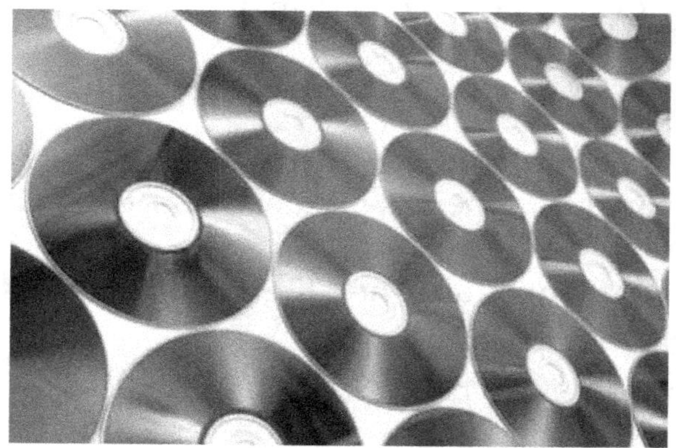

Create a backup, then. This may involve cloning to a CD, DVD, or external hard drive. If you store on CD or DVD, remember that you may need to copy to a new CD or DVD every five years. They have the longest shelf life when stored vertically in a cool area of the home.

If you frequently upload photos, you may wish to invest in a memory card reader. A memory card reader can be permanently connected to a computer and allows for quicker uploading.

Photo managing software:

After organizing your photographs on your computer, you may wish to transfer copies to photo management software. You may have already received excellent software with your camera, or you may choose to use Google's free Picasa or Adobe Photoshop Elements.

One advantage of using a photo manager is that you can add keywords to your photos. This could save you a great deal of time if you wind up with thousands of photographs. Then, when searching for a particular image, you simply enter keywords into your computer's search bar to retrieve all relevant images.

A further significant advantage is that many of these photo managers allow you to view the meta tags that your camera records, allowing you to view the settings you used to take a particular photograph. Some photographers use a photo manager like Picasa exclusively for photo management and an editor exclusively for photo modification. Others use both terms interchangeably. The best course of action is to research them online and read about each option you are contemplating. Or perhaps the one on your computer is the ideal match! In the next chapter, we will examine photo processors.

Photo Editing and Manipulation

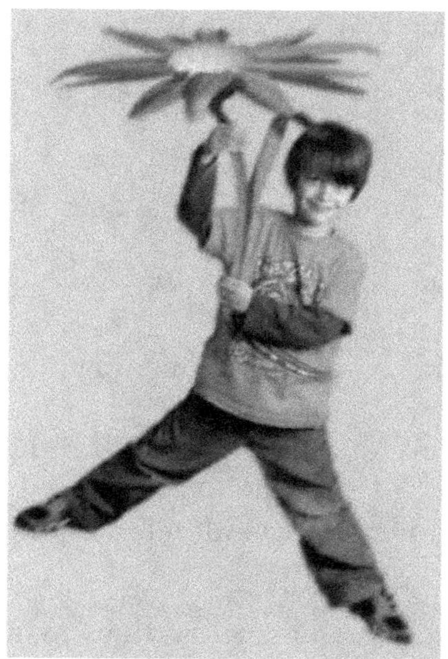

Photo Magic:

The term "image editing" encompasses every modification that can be made to a photograph, whether in a darkroom with film or on a computer with digital.

In the days of film, photo manipulation was referred to as "trick photography" and consisted of a variety of outlandish and amusing techniques, such as swapping the heads of people and backgrounds, as well as other such maneuvers. To view some amusing examples, please visit National Geographic Photo Foolery.

Photographers manipulated images in the past using techniques such as retouching with ink or paint, double exposure, and stitching together photographs or negatives in the darkroom.

In the digital darkroom, your camera has already performed a portion of the processing, leaving you with the enjoyable part, and due to Adobe Photoshop Elements and many other software programs, you can be much more creative than film photographers can be in their dark rooms.

It is acceptable to only possess the most fundamental photo modification software. What you are learning about photography will serve you well. And nowadays, the majority of fundamental editing programs enable you to edit in many of the ways we will discuss in this chapter.

Then, when you are prepared to advance, contemplate the following:

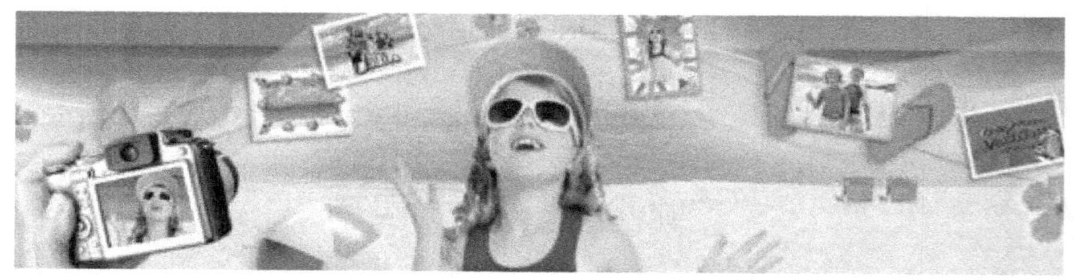

- **Photoshop Elements by Adobe:**

The market champion in photo editing and manipulation, it is more user-friendly and less expensive (approximately $80) than its larger sibling, Photoshop CS4, which graphic artists spend years mastering (approximately $600). Check their website for a free download of a trial version.

- **Paint Shop Professional:**

It costs roughly the same as Photoshop Elements and is a close competitor. They offer complimentary 30-day trials too frequently. A number of photographers compare Paint Pro to Photoshop CS4.

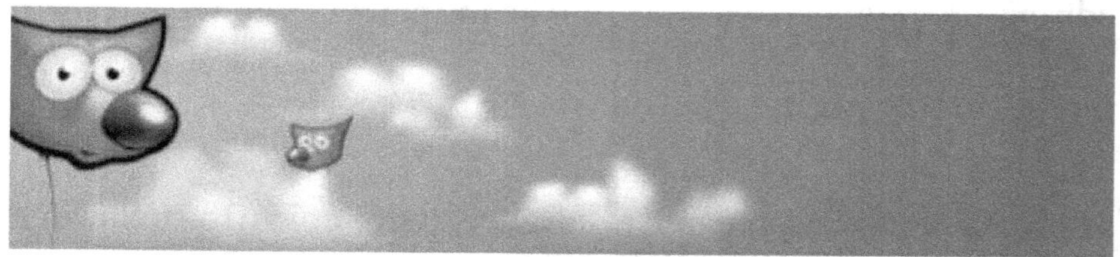

- **Using the GIMP:**

The GNU Image Manipulation Program is an unusual name for such a potent program. The acronym stands for GNU Image Manipulation Program. This freeware is continually advancing. It is available for Unix and Linux platforms, in addition to Windows (NT4/2000/XP/Vista) and Mac OS X. Some reviews have compared it to Photoshop.

In contrast to fundamental editors, such as Picasa, which only permit global adjustments, the aforementioned three and others like them offer the ability to perform spot corrections.

- **Google's Picasa:**

Google's Picasa, which is utilized by many as a photo manager and online photo album, is also a photo editor. This allows you to modify a photo in your online photo album without having to transfer it back and forth between the photo album and the editor. Quite interesting. And it's gratis.

Picasa provides fundamental editing tools, such as retouch, for removing defects, marks, etc. Like most editors, red-eye removal is included. It also has entertaining applications, such as the ability to create photo screensavers and integration with Google Earth.

To get the most out of your photo editor, consult its guide or help sections for an overview of its capabilities, and then read the documentation for any new applications that aren't completely intuitive.

You will be astonished at the wonders you can create with your photographs if you are willing to invest some time. For instance, the following are a few of the things you can do:

- **Crop:**

When you crop a photo, the editor does not automatically reduce its size; rather, it replaces the cropped pixels with pixels from the remaining image. This is essentially how digital zoom operates, which is why optical zoom provides superior image quality.

However, cropping can be extremely useful. The secret is to begin with a large number of pixels (tune your camera to the maximum resolution) and to never enlarge the image after cropping.

- **Adjust size:**

In contrast to cropping, resizing maintains the same number of pixels and resolution while allowing you to alter the dimensions. Photo editors also offer the option to maintain the aspect ratio, which means that when you alter either the height or the width, the other dimension is automatically adjusted to maintain the same proportion. If you fail to do so, your image will become distorted.

If the image is for a website, you should not have a resolution that is too high because it will increase the time it takes for the page to load.

Photoshop and other sophisticated photo editors have a function that allows you to optimize your image for the web by reducing its resolution and file size, if desired. Photoshop provides previews of various resolution sizes along with the download time.

- **Correct underexposed or overexposed areas of a photograph:**

Even the most fundamental photo editors allow you to adjust the exposure of an underexposed or overexposed image. Selecting shadows, highlights, and midtones allows you to selectively lighten or darken particular areas.

- **Accurate Colors:**

You can also fix colors that didn't come out correctly or use colors to create amusing images. The majority of photo editors allow you to manually modify tints and saturation, and some of the better ones also enable you to adjust white balance.

- **Translucent Backgrounds:**

Now that you've taken a substantial number of photographs, you undoubtedly realize how irritating background debris can be.

Photoshop Elements, Paintshop Pro, and GIMP all offer applications for background blurring. You can minimize the appearance of the background by following these steps:

1. Click on the photo after opening it to enter editing mode.

2. Soft Focus can be selected by clicking the Effects heading and selecting the Soft Focus option.

3. Adjust the size and amount sliders by moving the green crosshairs to the center of the point of focus and then dragging the size and amount sliders.

- **Retouching and additional amusements:**

All sophisticated photo editors, such as PS Elements, etc., allow you to clone out imperfections, creases, errant branches, logos, and anything else you don't want in the image. The cloning technique entails selecting pixels from a photograph and pasting them over a target area. This can be a tedious procedure.

However, Picasa has a similar retouching function that operates on the same principle but is significantly simpler to use. In Picasa, you click on the area you wish to modify and then click on the portion of the same image you wish to use as a replacement.

Picasa then automatically combines the borders, making the procedure much faster.

although you cannot anticipate the same level of perfection as from the industry giants. However, with Picasa, you can rapidly change things such as cheekbones and eyes, resulting in a great deal of laughter, particularly if you have children.

- **Theatrical Effects:**

With a photo editor, a variety of special effects can be created. For instance, you can transform a photograph into an impressionistic painting. To capture tones, lines, and highlights without the distraction of color, you can convert a color photograph to black and white.

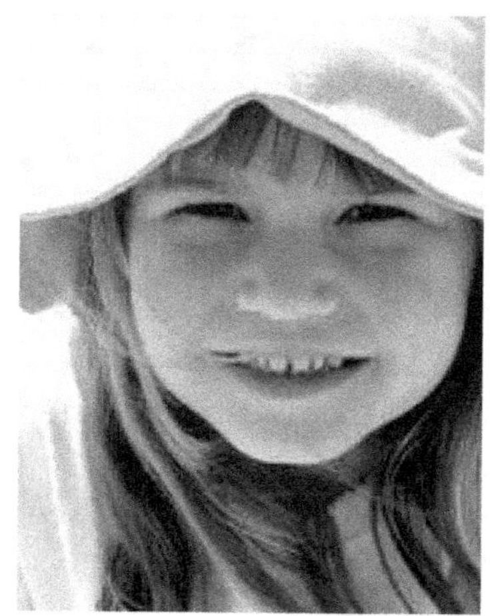

You may also choose sepia for a vintage appearance. These are only a few of the many available special effects.

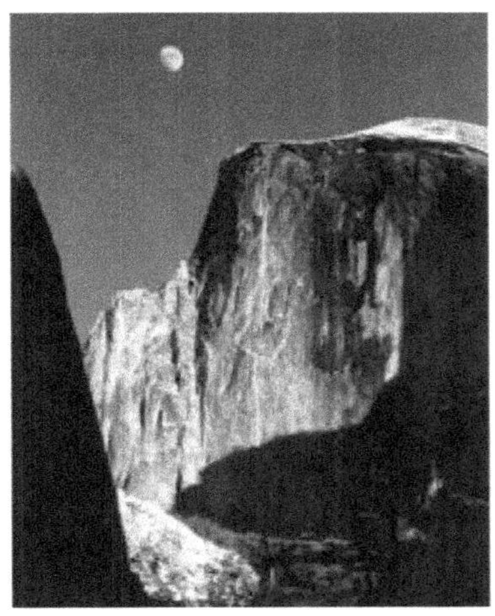

- **Noise Abatement:**

In the same way that using an ISO setting that is too high can cause digital noise, excessive photo editing can also result in digital noise. Occasionally, there is simply no way to get the picture and avoid commotion. Noise Ninja is here to help! You can find free software that performs adequately online, but if you're publishing an 8-by-10 or submitting the photo to a stock photo website, you may need something more robust. Noise Ninja is one of the most prominent noise reduction programs among professional photographers.

- **Warning:**

The more times you save a JPEG image during image modification, the more fidelity you lose. If the photo is significant to you, make a replica and alter the copy instead of the original.

Share your images.

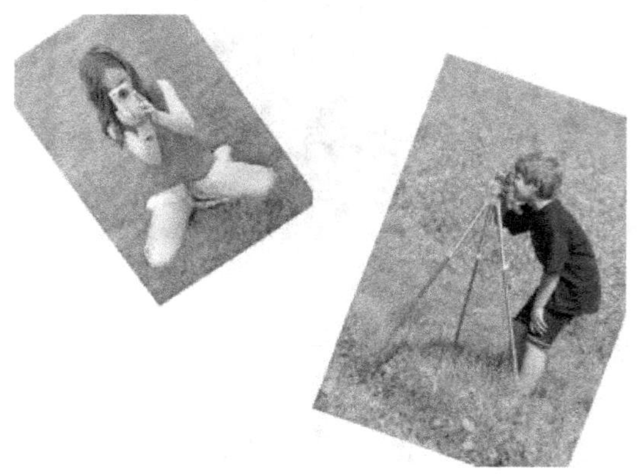

Digital photography allows you to share your photographs in a variety of formats, including print, online photo albums, email, and websites. Images can also be printed for use in school assignments, such as reports and crafts.

The practice of printing:

Whether you're printing a large poster for your room, an 8x10 portrait for framing, or photographs for your pocketbook, here are a few tips for printing your photos. (Be careful to consult your printer's manual and software documentation.)

- **The decision:**

If you have resized a photocopy, you may need to print the original. For example, most inkjet printers perform optimally at 200 dpi. If you submit a photo with a resolution of 300 or 150 dpi, the quality will not be as excellent. Check your manual or the manufacturer's website for recommendations. Then, using a photo editor, resample the images to the desired dpi. If in doubt, opt for 300 dpi.

- **The Paper:**

Utilize photo-printing paper, and if feasible, that which the manufacturer of your printer recommends for your model or model family. Use specialty paper for greeting card endeavors. Both are available online and in a variety of office supply and arts and crafts stores. Numerous photo software companies make it simple to order print duplicates online, but you will typically save money by publishing your own photos. Local printing is an alternative option. Typically, this is as simple as messaging them your photos.

Sharing on the Internet

There are numerous free websites that enable you to create online photo galleries and share them with friends and family.

- **Websites and groups for photo sharing:**

Google's free Picasa program is one of the finest and most widely used. Similar to Picasa, many of these allow you to secure your albums and set a password so that only the people you want to view your photographs can do so.

Alternatively, you can share your photos through an online community such as Flickr. Flickr requires its users to designate their own photos as either secure, moderate, or restricted. Here, you can also receive and provide feedback on your photos. Due to age requirements, you may need parental assistance with this task. At SurfNetKids.com, you and your parents can read evaluations of these photo-sharing websites.

- **Emailing Images:**

Emailing your photos to family and friends is another method of sharing them online. Before sending an email, be sure to create a copy that is the appropriate size for the email. Everything above 400 pixels necessitates horizontal navigation. If your image editor allows you to resample the image, you should do so because you do not need all those additional pixels. Then, open your email, select the "attachment" option, and navigate to your photo subdirectory. Click the file to transmit it. If you are uploading images to a blog or website, try to limit their width to between 300 and 400 pixels, or use thumbnails that link to a larger image that is not so large that it requires navigating to view the entire image. Be sure to reduce the number of pixels so that your web pages render quickly.

Photoshop Elements and a few other programs enable you to do so without discernible quality degradation.

Photo Crafts and Presents:

Using your photos and a printer, you can make some very interesting creations.

Here are a few examples:

- Christmas cards

- CD Sleeves

- Identifying marks

- Transfers applied to T-shirts

- Picture Quilts

- Image calendars

CONCLUSION

As we reach the final chapter of "Through the Eyes of Young Shutterbugs: A Digital Camera Guide for Kids," it's clear that this journey has been about much more than mastering the art of photography. It's been a voyage of self-discovery, creative expression, and empowerment. From the very first click of the shutter to the mesmerizing images that now grace these pages, our young readers have transformed into confident and capable photographers, armed with the skills to capture the world around them and share their unique stories.

In a world where technology often takes center stage, this guide aimed to remind us that technology can also be a powerful tool for self-expression and connection. Our young shutterbugs have learned to navigate the intricacies of digital cameras, lighting, composition, and post-processing, but they've also embraced the notion that a photograph is more than just a visual record—it's a reflection of their thoughts, emotions, and perspectives. Through their lenses, they've painted vivid portraits of their lives, experiences, and dreams.

As we bid farewell to these pages, let's carry the lessons of this book forward. Let's remember that creativity knows no bounds, and that every moment presents an opportunity to capture something remarkable. Whether it's a sunbeam dancing on a leaf, the twinkle in a friend's eye, or the sweeping panorama of a breathtaking landscape, the world is an ever-evolving canvas waiting for these young artists to make their mark.

May "Through the Eyes of Young Shutterbugs" continue to inspire, not just as a guide to photography, but as a testament to the boundless potential that resides within each of us. May its readers embark on a lifelong journey of curiosity and exploration, armed with the knowledge that their voices matter and their perspectives are worth sharing.

So, let's pick up our cameras and keep chasing those fleeting moments, those vibrant stories, and those unexpected wonders. As the curtain falls on this book, a new begins—one where the world is seen through the eyes of empowered young shutterbugs, capturing

the essence of life, one click at a time.

www.ingramcontent.com/pod-product-compliance
Lightning Source LLC
Chambersburg PA
CBHW060100260726
48658CB00004B/1348